Microsoft® Office Word 2007

Level 3 (Second Edition)

Microsoft® Office Word 2007: Level 3 (Second Edition)

Part Number: 084895
Course Edition: 1.10

NOTICES

What is the Microsoft Business Certification Program?

The Microsoft Business Certification Program enables candidates to show that they have something exceptional to offer – proven expertise in Microsoft Office programs. The two certification tracks allow candidates to choose how they want to exhibit their skills, either through validating skills within a specific Microsoft product or taking their knowledge to the next level and combining Microsoft programs to show that they can apply multiple skill sets to complete more complex office tasks. Recognized by businesses and schools around the world, over 3 million certifications have been obtained in over 100 different countries. The Microsoft Business Certification Program is the only Microsoft-approved certification program of its kind.

What is the Microsoft Certified Application Specialist Certification?

The Microsoft Certified Application Specialist Certification exams focus on validating specific skill sets within each of the Microsoft® Office system programs. The candidate can choose which exam(s) they want to take according to which skills they want to validate. The available Application Specialist exams include:

- Using Microsoft® Windows Vista™
- Using Microsoft® Office Word 2007
- Using Microsoft® Office Excel® 2007
- Using Microsoft® Office PowerPoint® 2007
- Using Microsoft® Office Access 2007
- Using Microsoft® Office Outlook® 2007

What is the Microsoft Certified Application Professional Certification?

The Microsoft Certified Application Professional Certification exams focus on a candidate's ability to use the 2007 Microsoft® Office system to accomplish industry-agnostic functions, for example Budget Analysis and Forecasting, or Content Management and Collaboration. The available Application Professional exams currently include:

- Organizational Support
- Creating and Managing Presentations
- Content Management and Collaboration
- Budget Analysis and Forecasting

What do the Microsoft Business Certification Vendor of Approved Courseware logos represent?

The logos validate that the courseware has been approved by the Microsoft® Business Certification Vendor program and that these courses cover objectives that will be included in the relevant exam. It also means that after utilizing this courseware, you may be prepared to pass the exams required to become a Microsoft Certified Application Specialist or Microsoft Certified Application Professional.

For more information:

To learn more about Microsoft Certified Application Specialist or Professional exams, visit **www.microsoft.com/learning/msbc**.

To learn about other Microsoft Certified Application Specialist approved courseware from Element K, visit **www.elementkcourseware.com**.

∗ The availability of Microsoft Certified Application exams varies by Microsoft Office program, program version and language. Visit **www.microsoft.com/learning** for exam availability.

Microsoft, the Office Logo, Outlook, and PowerPoint are either registered trademarks or trademarks of Microsoft Corporation in the United States and/or other countries. The Microsoft Certified Application Specialist and Microsoft Certified Application Professional Logos are used under license from Microsoft Corporation.

Microsoft® Office Word 2007: Level 3 (Second Edition)

Lesson 5: Making Long Documents Easier to Use

Lesson 6: Securing a Document

Appendix A: Creating Forms

Appendix B: Using XML in Word

About This Course

You know to use Microsoft® Office Word 2007 to create and format typical business documents. Now, you may need to work on more complex documents. In this course, you will use Word to create, manage, revise, and distribute long documents and forms.

Microsoft® Office Word 2007 is much more than a word processing program. It can be used to save documents in a variety of other file formats, to collaborate on complicated business documents, and to manage how documents are accessed and distributed.

This course can also benefit you if you are preparing to take the Microsoft Certified Application Specialist exam for Microsoft® Word 2007. Please refer to the CD-ROM that came with this course for a document that maps exam objectives to the content in the Microsoft Office Word Courseware series. To access the mapping document, insert the CD-ROM into your CD-ROM drive and at the root of the ROM, double-click ExamMapping.doc to open the mapping document. In addition to the mapping document, two assessment files per course can be found on the CD-ROM to check your knowledge. To access the assessments, at the root of the course part number folder, double-click 084895s3.doc to view the assessments without the answers marked, or double-click 084895ie.doc to view the assessments with the answers marked.

Course Description

Target Student

This course is designed for persons who want to gain skills necessary to manage long documents, collaborate with others, and secure documents. In addition, it will be helpful for persons preparing for the Microsoft Certified Application Specialist exams for Microsoft® Office Word 2007.

Course Prerequisites

Students should be able to use Microsoft® Office Word 2007 to create, edit, format, save, and print business documents that contain text, tables, and graphics. Students should also be able to use a web browser and an email program. A basic understanding of XML would also be helpful. In order to understand how Word interacts with other applications in the Microsoft Office System, students should have a basic understanding of how worksheets and presentations work. To ensure success, you need to first take the following Element K courses or have equivalent knowledge:

- *Microsoft® Office Word 2007: Level 1*
- *Microsoft® Office Word 2007: Level 2*

If your book did not come with a CD, please go to **http://www.elementk.com/courseware-file-downloads** to download the data files.

How to Use This Book

As a Learning Guide

Each lesson covers one broad topic or set of related topics. Lessons are arranged in order of increasing proficiency with *Microsoft® Office Word 2007*; skills you acquire in one lesson are used and developed in subsequent lessons. For this reason, you should work through the lessons in sequence.

We organized each lesson into results-oriented topics. Topics include all the relevant and supporting information you need to master *Microsoft® Office Word 2007*, and activities allow you to apply this information to practical hands-on examples.

You have an opportunity to try out each new skill on a specially prepared sample file. This saves you typing time and allows you to concentrate on the skill at hand. Through the use of sample files, hands-on activities, illustrations that give you feedback at crucial steps, and supporting background information, this book provides you with the foundation and structure to learn *Microsoft® Office Word 2007* quickly and easily.

As a Review Tool

Any method of instruction is only as effective as the time and effort you are willing to invest in it. In addition, some of the information that you learn in class may not be important to you immediately, but it may become important later on. For this reason, we encourage you to spend some time reviewing the topics and activities after the course. For additional challenge when reviewing activities, try the "What You Do" column before looking at the "How You Do It" column.

As a Reference

The organization and layout of the book make it easy to use as a learning tool and as an after-class reference. You can use this book as a first source for definitions of terms, background information on given topics, and summaries of procedures.

Course Icons

Icon	Description
	A **Caution Note** makes students aware of potential negative consequences of an action, setting, or decision that are not easily known.
	Display Slide provides a prompt to the instructor to display a specific slide. Display Slides are included in the Instructor Guide only.
	An **Instructor Note** is a comment to the instructor regarding delivery, classroom strategy, classroom tools, exceptions, and other special considerations. Instructor Notes are included in the Instructor Guide only.
	Notes Page indicates a page that has been left intentionally blank for students to write on.
	A **Student Note** provides additional information, guidance, or hints about a topic or task.
	A **Version Note** indicates information necessary for a specific version of software.

Certification

This course is designed to help you prepare for the following certification.

Certification Path: Microsoft Certified Application Specialist – Word 2007

This course is one of a series of Element K courseware titles that addresses Microsoft Certified Application Specialist (Microsoft Business Certification) skill sets. The Microsoft Certified Application Specialist program is for individuals who use Microsoft's business desktop software and who seek recognition for their expertise with specific Microsoft products. Certification candidates must pass one or more proficiency exams in order to earn Microsoft Certified Application Specialist certification.

Course Objectives

In this course, you will create, manage, revise, and distribute long documents.

You will:

- use Microsoft Office Word 2007 with other programs.
- collaborate on documents.
- manage document versions.
- add reference marks and notes.
- make long documents easier to use.
- secure a document.
- create forms.
- use XML in Word.

Course Requirements

Hardware

Classroom Computers

For this course, you will need one computer for each student and one for the instructor. Each computer will need the following minimum hardware components:

- A 1 GHz Pentium-class processor or faster.
- A minimum of 256 MB of RAM. 512 MB of RAM is recommended.
- A 10 GB hard disk or larger. You should have at least 1 GB of free hard disk space available for the Microsoft Office installation.
- A CD-ROM drive.
- A keyboard and mouse or other pointing device.
- A 1024 x 768 resolution monitor is recommended.
- Network cards and cabling for local network access.
- Internet access (contact your local network administrator).
- A printer (optional) or an installed printer driver.
- A projection system to display the instructor's computer screen.

Software

Classroom Computers

- Microsoft® Office Professional Edition 2007
- Microsoft Office Suite Service Pack 1
- Windows XP Professional with Service Pack 2

This course was developed using the Windows XP operating system; however, the manufacturer's documentation states that it will also run on Vista. If you use Vista, you might notice some slight differences when keying the course.

Class Setup

Initial Class Setup

1. Install Windows XP Professional on an empty partition.

   - Leave the Administrator password blank.
   - For all other installation parameters, use values that are appropriate for your environment (see your local network administrator for details).

2. On Windows XP Professional, disable the Welcome screen. (This step ensures that students will be able to log on as the Administrator user regardless of what other user accounts exist on the computer.)

   a. Click Start and choose Control Panel→User Accounts.

   b. Click Change The Way Users Log On And Off.

   c. Uncheck Use Welcome Screen.

   d. Click Apply Options.

3. On Windows XP Professional, install Service Pack 2. Use the Service Pack installation defaults.

4. On the computer, install a printer driver (a physical print device is optional). Click Start and choose Printers And Faxes. Under Printer Tasks, click Add A Printer and follow the prompts.

   If you do not have a physical printer installed, right-click the printer and choose Pause Printing to prevent any print error messages.

5. Run the Internet Connection Wizard to set up the Internet connection appropriately for your environment, if you did not do so during installation.

6. Display known file type extensions.

   a. Open Windows Explorer (right-click Start and then select Explore).

   b. Choose Tools→Folder Options.

   c. On the View tab, in the Advanced Settings list box, uncheck Hide Extensions For Known File Types.

   d. Click Apply, and then click OK.

   e. Close Windows Explorer.

7. Log on to the computer as the Administrator user if you have not already done so.

8. Perform a Complete installation of the Microsoft Office 2007 System.

9. In the User Name dialog box, click OK to accept the default user name and initials.

10. In the Microsoft Office 2007 Activation Wizard dialog box, click Next to activate the Office 2007 application.

11. When the activation of Microsoft Office 2007 is complete, click Close to close the Microsoft Office 2007 Activation Wizard dialog box.

12. In the User Name dialog box, click OK.

13. In the Welcome To Microsoft 2007! dialog box, click Finish. You must have an active Internet connection in order to complete this step. Here, you select the Download And Install Updates From Microsoft Update When Available (Recommended) option, so that whenever there is a new update, it gets automatically installed in your system.

14. After the Microsoft Update runs, in the Microsoft Office dialog box, click OK.

15. Perform a customized installation.

    a. Click + (plus sign) next to Office Tools.

    b. From the Microsoft Office Document Imaging drop-down list, select Run All From My Computer.

    c. Click Install Now.

    d. Click Close.

16. Minimize the Language Bar, if necessary.

17. On the course CD-ROM, open the 084_895 folder. Then, open the Data folder. Run the self-extracting file located in it named 084895dd.exe. This will install a folder named 084895Data on your C drive. This folder contains all the data files that you will use to complete this course.

    Within each lesson folder, you may find a Solution folder. This folder contains solution files for the lesson's activities and lesson lab, which can be used by students to check their end results.

If your book did not come with a CD, please go to **http:// www.elementk.com/ courseware-file-downloads** to download the data files.

Customize the Windows Desktop

Customize the Windows desktop to display the My Computer and My Network Places icons on the student and instructor systems by following these steps:

1. Right-click the Desktop and choose Properties.

2. Select the Desktop tab.

3. Click Customize Desktop.

4. In the Desktop Items dialog box, check My Computer and My Network Places.

5. Click OK and click Apply.

6. Close the Display Properties dialog box.

Create a Digital Certificate on Every Computer

Perform this setup procedure on every computer.

1. Choose Start→All Programs→Microsoft Office→Microsoft Office Tools→Digital Certificate For VBA Projects.

2. In the Create Digital Certificate dialog box, in the Your Certificate's Name text box, type a unique name for the certificate and click OK.

   It is recommended that you use a generic name such as Student01 on the first computer. Then, on the second computer, repeat this step and name the certificate Student02. Continue in this manner until each computer has one uniquely named digital certificate.

3. Click OK to close the success message box.

Before Every Class

1. Log on to the computer as the Administrator user.

2. Delete any existing data files from C:\084895Data.

3. Extract a fresh copy of the course data files from the CD-ROM provided with the course manual.

List of Additional Files

Printed with each activity is a list of files students open to complete that activity. Many activities also require additional files that students do not open, but are needed to support the file(s) students are working with. These supporting files are included with the student data files on the course CD-ROM or data disk. Do not delete these files.

1 | Using Microsoft® Office Word 2007 with Other Programs

Lesson Time: 1 hour(s)

Lesson Objectives:

In this lesson, you will use Microsoft Office Word 2007 with other programs.

You will:

- Link to an Excel 2007 worksheet.
- Link a chart to Excel data.
- Send a document outline to PowerPoint.
- Extract text from a fax.
- Send a document as an email message.

Introduction

You have used Microsoft® Office Word as a stand-alone application to create various types of documents. Now, you may need to use other programs to extend your capabilities beyond the scope of word processing. In this lesson, you will use Word with other applications such as Microsoft® Office Excel® and Microsoft® Office PowerPoint®.

Word can interact with other applications. Using this capability, you can use existing information in Word in other applications or vice versa. This ensures that the data you use is consistent and accurate.

TOPIC A

Link to a Microsoft® Office Excel® 2007 Worksheet

You are familiar with creating and customizing information in a Word document. In the course of your work, you may need to use information from other applications while ensuring that the information stays current. In this topic, you will link to data in an Excel worksheet.

Assume that you need to create a table in Word using data from an Excel worksheet. Rather than retyping the data, risking typographical errors, you can create a dynamic link to the Excel worksheet containing the desired data. This way, you will avoid data entry mistakes and ensure that any updates done on the source worksheet are reflected in the Word document.

Data Linking

Data linking is the process of linking a textual or pictorial object to a data source. When an object is linked to a source, the data remains stored in the source. A replica of the source information is displayed in the object. This way, when the source is updated, the linked object also gets automatically updated. Data linking helps maintain consistency between a data source and the linked object while keeping the data up to date.

How to Link to an Excel 2007 Worksheet

Procedure Reference: Link to Data in an Excel Sheet

To link to data in an Excel sheet:

1. Open the Word document in which you want to create a linked object and the Excel worksheet that contains the source data you want to create a link to.
2. In the Word document, select a location for the linked object.
3. If necessary, switch to the Excel worksheet.
4. Select the entire worksheet, a range of cells, or the object that you want to copy.
5. Copy the selected content.
6. Switch to the Word document and on the Home tab, in the Clipboard group, click the Paste drop-down arrow and choose Paste Special to launch the Paste Special dialog box.
7. Select the Paste Link option.
8. In the As list box, select Microsoft Office Excel Worksheet Object.
9. Click OK to link to the content selected in the Excel sheet.

Procedure Reference: Modify Information in a Linked Worksheet Object

To modify information in a linked worksheet object:

1. Display the data source.
   - Double-click the linked worksheet object.
   - Or, right-click the linked worksheet object and choose Linked Worksheet Object→ Open Link.
2. Modify data in the source file, as desired.
3. Switch to the Word document.

4. Right-click the linked worksheet object and choose Update Link to update the linked worksheet object.

Obsolete Links

Over the course of a document's lifecycle, you may find that some links are no longer relevant and should be removed from the document. This can be done by breaking the obsolete links.

Procedure Reference: Break an Obsolete Link

To break a link:

1. Right-click the linked object and choose Linked Worksheet Object→Links to display the Links dialog box.
2. In the Links list box, select the desired linked worksheet object.
3. Click Break Link and then click Yes.
4. Click OK to close the Links dialog box.

ACTIVITY 1-1

Linking a Document to an Excel Worksheet

Data Files:

Monthly Numbers Memo.docx, Monthly Sales Data.xlsx

Before You Begin:

From the C:\084895Data\Using Word 2007 with Other Programs folder, open Monthly Numbers Memo.docx and Monthly Sales Data.xlsx.

Scenario:

You are ready to send the memo on sales data. The last time you circulated the memo, some realtors replied saying there was not enough information. They would like to see the most current monthly sales numbers for each office.

What You Do	How You Do It
1. **Insert the linked worksheet object.**	a. **Save the Excel worksheet as *My Monthly Sales Data.xlsx* and the Word document as *My Monthly Numbers Memo.docx***
	b. **Scroll down and place the insertion point at the end of the Word document.**
	c. In the Excel window, **copy cells A3 through E6.**
	d. In the Word window, on the Home tab, in the Clipboard group, **click the Paste drop-down arrow and choose Paste Special** to open the Paste Special dialog box.
	e. **Select the Paste Link option.**
	f. In the As list box, **select Microsoft Office Excel Worksheet Object and click OK** to insert the linked Excel object.
2. **Update the linked object with the March numbers.**	a. **Double-click the linked worksheet object** to display the My Monthly Sales Data.xlsx file.
	b. In cell B6, **type *4.1*** to include the March data for the North office **and press Tab** to move to the next cell.
	c. **Include the March data for the South and East offices as 5.3 and 6.0, respectively.**
	d. In the Word window, **right-click the linked worksheet object and choose Update Link.**

TOPIC B

Link a Chart to Excel Data

You have used Word to link to data in an Excel worksheet. Similarly, you can create charts in your document based on external data and also keep them current. In this topic, you will link data in an Excel worksheet to a chart.

After distributing the weekly sales meeting handout, you notice that the chart in the handout doesn't match the data in the corresponding table. Had you created a link between the chart and the Excel worksheet, the chart would have been automatically updated.

How to Link a Chart to Excel Data

Procedure Reference: Link a Chart to Excel Data

To link a chart to Excel data:

1. In the Word document, click where you want the copied information to be displayed.
2. On the Insert tab, in the Illustrations group, click Chart and choose the desired chart type.
3. In the Chart In Microsoft Office Word – Microsoft Excel window, select the existing data in the worksheet.
4. Copy the required data in the worksheet.
5. Switch to the Chart In Microsoft Office Word — Microsoft Excel window.
6. On the Home tab, in the Clipboard group, click the Paste drop-down arrow and choose Paste Special to launch the Paste Special dialog box.
7. Click OK to link to the content selected in the Excel sheet.
8. If necessary, in Word, right-click the chart and choose Edit Data to edit the data in the worksheet.
9. Close the Chart In Microsoft Office Word – Microsoft Excel window.

ACTIVITY 1-2

Linking a Chart to Excel Data

Before You Begin:
My Monthly Sales Data.xlsx and My Monthly Numbers Memo.docx are open.

Scenario:
In the sales data memo you sent, you forgot to update the chart to reflect the most current data. To avoid this in the future, you want to link the chart to the data maintained in Excel.

What You Do	How You Do It
1. **Create a linked worksheet object in the Word document.**	a. **Place the insertion point at the end of the Word document.**
	b. On the Insert tab, in the Illustrations group, **click Chart and then click OK** to create a Clustered Column chart.
	c. In the Chart In Microsoft Office Word – Microsoft Excel window, **select cells A2 to D5.**
2. In the Excel worksheet, **copy the January to March data for the North, South, and East regions.**	a. **Switch to the My Monthly Sales Data.xlsx worksheet.**
	b. **Copy cells A3 through E6.**
	c. On the View tab, in the Window group, **click Switch Windows and choose Chart In Microsoft Office Word** to restore the Chart In Microsoft Office Word window.
	d. On the Home tab, in the Clipboard group, **click the Paste drop-down arrow and choose Paste Special** to open the Paste Special dialog box.
	e. **Click OK** to insert the chart.

3. **Open the Chart In Microsoft Office Word window** to update it.

a. **Restore the Word window.**

b. **Right-click the chart and choose Edit Data** to switch to the Chart In Microsoft Office Word – Microsoft Excel window.

c. In cell B4, **select the number 2.1, type *4.0* and press Tab.**

d. **Restore the Word document** and notice the data is updated in the chart in Word.

e. **Save the Word document and the Excel worksheet.**

f. **Close all open files and Excel.**

TOPIC C

Send a Document Outline to Microsoft® Office PowerPoint®

Not only can Word receive information from other programs, but it can also provide information to other programs. In this topic, you will use an existing Word document outline to create a new Microsoft® Office PowerPoint® presentation.

When creating a PowerPoint presentation based on an existing Word document, you could start creating the presentation with a blank slide—adding slides, typing titles, and entering bullet points. However, this is time-consuming and leaves room for error. A better method is to send an existing Word document to PowerPoint to automatically create the new presentation.

Outline View

The purpose of Word's Outline view is to show how a document's contents are organized. You can reorganize the content in the document using the tools in the Outline Tools group. The Outline Tools group can be accessed on the Outlining tab.

Heading Styles and Slides

A document's headings determine where the heading text will be placed in a PowerPoint slide. When a document's outline is sent to PowerPoint, text formatted with the Heading 1 style becomes a new slide's title. Text formatted with the Heading 2 style becomes a first-level bullet point. Each subsequent heading level in the document corresponds with a bullet point level in a slide.

Levels

Levels are a way to organize the visibility of content in a presentation. From the Show Level drop-down list, you can select which levels to show in the presentation. The selected level and all higher levels will be visible.

How to Send a Document Outline to PowerPoint

Procedure Reference: Send a Document Outline to PowerPoint

To send a document outline to PowerPoint:

1. In the Microsoft Office Status Bar, click the Outline button to display the document in Outline view and verify whether the headings are displayed at the appropriate levels.

2. If necessary, add the Send To Microsoft Office PowerPoint button to the Quick Access toolbar.

3. On the Quick Access toolbar, click the Send To Microsoft Office PowerPoint button.

4. Press the Page Down or Page Up key to review the slides to make sure they appear as intended.

5. If necessary, make modifications.

6. Save the presentation.

ACTIVITY 1-3

Sending a Document Outline to PowerPoint

Data Files:

Stockholder Report.docx

Before You Begin:

From the C:\084895Data\Using Word 2007 with Other Programs folder, open Stockholder Report.docx.

Scenario:

Your manager has asked you to create a PowerPoint presentation based on the latest stockholder report. She needs it quickly, so you need to use the most efficient method in order to generate the presentation.

What You Do	How You Do It
1. **Display the report in Outline view.**	a. In the Microsoft Office Status Bar, **click the Outline button** [icon] to switch to Outline view.
	b. On the Outlining tab, in the Outline Tools group, from the Show Level drop-down list, **select Level 3.**
2. **Generate the PowerPoint presentation.**	a. **Add the Send To Microsoft Office PowerPoint command to the Quick Access toolbar.**
	b. On the Quick Access toolbar, **click the Send To PowerPoint button** [icon] to create a PowerPoint presentation based on the document's outline.
	c. **Review the slides by pressing Page Down until the last slide is displayed.**
	d. **Save the presentation as *My Stockholder Report.pptx* and the document as *My Stockholder Report.docx*.**
	e. **Close all open windows.**

TOPIC D
Extract Text from a Fax

When you receive a document, it is easy to reuse the content in another application, such as PowerPoint. However, when you receive a fax, typically you need to retype the text you want to use. In this topic, you will extract text from a fax and add it to a document.

A salesperson faxes a new customer sheet to you and wants you to type that information into a Word document. If you can transfer the text from the fax file directly to a Word document, you can save time and effort and avoid errors that may occur when doing the task manually.

Microsoft Office Document Imaging

Microsoft Office Document Imaging is a feature that is used to view and manipulate scanned documents and digitally received faxes. It uses Optical Character Recognition (OCR) technology to extract text from a scanned or faxed image and export it to Word.

 Optical Character Recognition (OCR) is a technology that allows you to convert digitized information into an editable format.

How to Extract Text from a Fax
Procedure Reference: Extract Text from a Fax File

To extract text from a fax file:

1. Choose Start→All Programs→Microsoft Office→Microsoft Office Tools→Microsoft Office Document Imaging.
2. Open the desired fax file.
3. If necessary, select values from the Zoom drop-down list to adjust the view as needed.
4. Select the specific text you want to extract.
5. Send the text to a new document.
    *   Choose Tools→Send Text To Word.
    *   Or, on the Standard toolbar, click the Send Text To Word button.
6. In the Send Text To Word dialog box, click OK.
7. In the Microsoft Office Document Imaging message box, click OK.
8. If necessary, edit and format the extracted text in the new Word document.
9. Save the Word document.

ACTIVITY 1-4

Extracting Text from a Fax File

Data Files:

Newsletter Fax.tif

Scenario:

You have received a one-page fax from a writer who contributes to your department's monthly newsletter. The fax includes his story about a website. You need that story in a Word document, but you don't have the time to retype it.

What You Do	How You Do It
1. Open the fax in the Microsoft Office Document Imaging window.	a. **Choose Start→All Programs→Microsoft Office→Microsoft Office Tools→ Microsoft Office Document Imaging.**
	b. On the Standard toolbar, **click the Open button.**
	c. In the Open dialog box, **navigate to C:\084895Data\Using Word 2007 with Other Programs and double-click Newsletter Fax.tif** to open it.

2. **Send the story text to Word.**

a. From the Zoom drop-down list, **select Text Width.**

b. **Scroll down to the end of the page.**

c. With the Select tool active, **drag a selection area around the story text.**

d. **Choose Tools→Send Text To Word.**

e. In the Send Text To Word dialog box, **verify that the Current Selection option is selected and click OK two times.**

f. **Display the Save As dialog box** and, in the Save As Type drop-down list, **select Word Document (*.docx).**

g. In the File Name text box, **select the existing text, type** *My Newsletters Fax* **and click Save.**

h. **Close the Word document and then close the fax document without saving the changes.**

i. **Close all open windows.**

TOPIC E
Send a Document as an Email Message

You know how to extract text from a fax. Once you have the desired content in a document, you may need to send a copy of that document to someone else. Rather than put it on a disk or a network location, you can send it as an email message. In this topic, you will send a document as an email message.

Your manager, who is on a business trip, is calling to say that she needs you to send her last year's budget review document to help defend her proposal. Instead of wasting time and money sending the document by overnight mail, you simply email the document to her.

How to Send a Document as an Email Message

Procedure Reference: Send a Document as an Email Message

To send a document as an email message:

1. Open the desired document.
2. If necessary, add the Send To Mail Recipient command to the Quick Access toolbar.
3. On the Quick Access toolbar, click the Send To Mail Recipient button.
4. In the To text box, type the email address(es) of the primary mail recipient(s).

 Separate multiple recipient addresses with semicolons.

5. If necessary, in the Cc text box, type the email address(es) of the recipient(s) you want to copy in on the email.
6. In the Subject text box, type the subject of the email.
7. If necessary, in the Introduction text box, type an introduction.
8. Click Send A Copy.

DISCOVERY ACTIVITY 1-5

Sending a Document as an Email Message

Data Files:

Sending an Email Message.exe

Setup:

This is a simulated activity that requires Microsoft Exchange Server 2007 and Microsoft® Office Outlook®. In this simulation, your editor has an email account address of: mcoleman@company.internal.com.

Scenario:

The newsletter's editor is home with a cold, but she said she could read through the economics site story if you send it to her.

1. To launch the simulation, **browse to the C:\084895Data\Using Word 2007 with Other Programs\Simulations folder.**

2. **Double-click the Sending an Email Message.exe file.**

3. **Maximize the simulation window.**

4. **Follow the on-screen steps for the simulation.**

5. When you have finished the activity, **close the simulation window.**

Lesson 1 Follow-up

In this lesson, you used Word to link to and extract information from other programs. Utilizing Word's ability to interact with other programs will help you to reuse existing content, prevent you from needlessly retyping information, and help to maintain consistency between data sources and documents.

1. **On your job, how will you use Word with other programs?**

2. **Which of the tools do you think you will find most valuable? Why?**

2 | Collaborating on Documents

Lesson Time: 1 hour(s), 25 minutes

Lesson Objectives:

In this lesson, you will collaborate on documents.

You will:

- Modify user information.
- Send a document for review.
- Review a document.
- Compare document changes.
- Merge two documents.
- Review track changes and comments.

Introduction

You interacted with other programs using Microsoft® Office Word 2007. Once you finish work on your document, you may need to share it with other people for feedback. In this lesson, you will collaborate on documents.

You received your document back from editing, and it is a jumbled mess. There are multicolored, handwritten marks everywhere, which are nearly illegible making the edits look challenging and time consuming. With Word, changes can be made and tracked directly in the document so that the edits are readable and easily identifiable.

TOPIC A
Modify User Information

When working in a collaborative environment, it is imperative that Word tracks who is changing a document. In this topic, you will provide Word with that information.

You have been asked to fill in on a project because the original author was reassigned. Since an editor will review the document, you need to modify the user information so you can be clearly identified as the person who worked on the document, making the collaboration process easier.

The Collaboration Process

The *collaboration* process is the interaction between two or more people working toward achieving a common goal. Collaborating on a document usually occurs in stages.

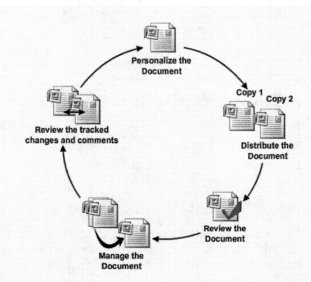

Figure 2-1: *The collaboration process.*

The following table describes each stage of the collaboration process.

Stage	Description
Personalize the document	Include user information that identifies you as the author of a document or a person who has worked on it.
Distribute the document	Distribute the document to those collaborating on it with you.
Review the document	Modify the document, as needed, by enabling track changes and inserting comments. Then, return the document.
Manage the document	Compare and merge the document changes into a single document.
Review the tracked changes and comments	Review the changes, accepting and rejecting them, as needed. If necessary, begin the collaboration process again.

The Document Information Panel

The Document Information panel appears above the document a user is working on. It gives you basic details about a document, such as the author name, title, subject, and keywords, that help to identify a document. The properties in the Document Information panel, such as metadata, can be automatically synchronized with the document content. You can also customize the Document Information panel by adding or removing document properties.

The Properties Dialog Box of a Document

The document's Properties dialog box consists of various tabs including General, Summary, Statistics, Contents, and Custom.

Tab	Contains Information On
General	File name and size; type of document; when the file was created, modified, and last accessed; and any file attributes.
Summary	Title, subject, author, manager, company, category, keywords, comments, and the hyperlink base of a document.
Statistics	When the file was created, modified, last accessed, and printed; who last saved the document; the revision number; the total editing time; and word count statistics.
Contents	The document contents.
Custom	Built-in and custom fields you can use to include a wider variety of information about the document.

How to Modify User Information

Procedure Reference: View the Automatically Updated Properties for a Document

To view the automatically updated properties for a document:

1. Click the Office button and choose Prepare→Properties.
2. In the Document Information panel, click Document Properties and choose Advanced Properties.
3. In the [document] Properties dialog box, select the desired tab to view the values for each of the properties.
4. Click OK.

Procedure Reference: Modify User Information

To modify user information:

1. Display the Word Options dialog box.
2. With the Popular category selected, in the Personalize Your Copy Of Microsoft Office section, in the User Name text box, type the name you want to use to identify yourself to other collaborators.
3. In the Initials text box, type the initials to be displayed.
4. Click OK.

The user information you type in Word becomes your user information for all Office 2007 programs.

ACTIVITY 2-1

Modifying User Information

Data Files:

Management Team.docx

Before You Begin:

From the C:\084895Data\Collaborating on Documents folder, open Management Team.docx.

Scenario:

You have been assigned to work on the Management Team document on a temporary basis. Since the document is part of a larger collaborative process, you have been asked to update your user information so that the changes you make to the document are attributable to you.

What You Do	How You Do It
1. Check the existing user name.	a. **Click the Office button and choose Prepare→Properties.**
	b. In the Document Information panel, observe that the name Justine Altman is displayed in the Author text box. **Click Document Properties and choose Advanced Properties.**
	c. In the Properties dialog box, **select the Statistics tab.**
	d. Notice that the Last Saved By property is set to the author of the document.
	e. **Click OK.**
2. Change the user name and initials.	a. **Display the Word Options dialog box.**
	b. With the Popular category selected, in the Personalize Your Copy Of Microsoft Office section, in the User Name text box, **type your name and press Tab.**
	c. In the Initials text box, **type your initials.**
	d. **Click OK.**

3. **Update the document with the necessary information.**

    a. **Scroll down, place the insertion point at the end of the third bullet point, and press Enter.**

    b. **Type *Brian Rodriguez, President, Southern Region***

    c. Under the "Relocation Services" heading, in the first line, **double-click the word "three" and type *four***

    d. **Save the document as *My Management Team.docx***

4. **Verify whether the user name value for the Last Saved By property is updated.**

    a. **Display the Properties dialog box.**

    b. On the Statistics tab, **view the change in the Last Saved By property.**

    c. **Click OK.**

    d. **Save and close the document.**

    e. **Close the Document Information panel.**

TOPIC B
Send a Document for Review

You personalized a document by modifying user information. So far, you have worked on documents by yourself, but your new project requires other team members to review your documents. In this topic, you will send a document for review.

Your document is ready for the project team to review. Instead of handing out paper copies to the project team, sending the document for review by email is a convenient way to distribute the document and helps you keep track of who has reviewed the document.

How to Send a Document for Review
Procedure Reference: Send a Document as an Attachment

To send a document as an attachment:
1. Open the desired document.
2. Click the Office button and choose Send→E-mail to display the document's Message window.
3. In the To text box, type the email address(es) of the primary mail recipient(s).
4. If necessary, in the Cc text box, type the email address(es) of the recipient(s) you want to copy in on the email.
5. In the Subject text box, type the subject of the email.
6. If necessary, type a message in the body of the email.
7. Click Send.

 Depending on how Outlook is set up, you may need to launch it and click the Send/Receive button to send the document for review.

DISCOVERY ACTIVITY 2-2

Sending a Document as an Attachment

Data Files:

Sending an Email Attachment_guided.exe

Setup:

This is a simulated activity that requires Microsoft Exchange Server 2007 and Microsoft Office Outlook. In this simulation, your editors are Mary Coleman and Sue Roe, and their email addresses are mcoleman@xchg.com and sroe@xchg.com, respectively. Your manager is Todd Lite and his email address is tlite@xchg.com.

Scenario:

Now that the Team document is complete, you need to send it for review. You require feedback for this document by the end of next week, but you aren't sure who will be editing the document. So, you decide to mail it to the two editors in your project team and also copy in your manager on the document.

1. To launch the simulation, **browse to the C:\084895Data\Collaborating on Documents\ Simulations folder.**

2. **Double-click the Sending an Email Attachment_guided.exe file.**

3. **Maximize the simulation window.**

4. **Follow the on-screen steps for the simulation.**

5. When you have finished the activity, **close the simulation window.**

TOPIC C
Review a Document

You know how to send documents for review. During a document's review, you may want to keep track of the changes made to a document or explain why some changes were made. In this topic, you will track changes to a document.

One of the reviewers of your document brings her hard copy to your desk, stating that she doesn't have time to mark up the document properly. Though she proceeds to tell you all of the edits she found, you are distracted and are only able to write down half of the things she's telling you. Had she marked the changes in the document electronically, you wouldn't have missed any of her suggestions.

The Track Changes Option

The Track Changes option in the Tracking group on the Review tab contains options that allow you to identify document modifications and the person who made those modifications. The following table describes the different options available in the Track Changes feature.

Option	Used To
Track Changes	Enable or disable track changes.
Change Tracking Options	Customize the appearance of the editing markup and comments using the Track Changes Options dialog box.
Change User Name	Display the Word Options dialog box that can be used to change the user information provided.

 With the help of the Track Changes indicator, you can identify whether the Track Changes feature is on. You can enable the indicator by right-clicking the status bar and choosing Track Changes.

The Track Changes Options Dialog Box

The Track Changes Options dialog box allows you to customize the appearance of edited content in a document.

Each of the sections in the Track Changes Options dialog box is described in the following table.

Section	Used To
Markup	Format insertions, deletions, line alignment, and comments.
Moves	Format and track the different move actions.
Table Cell High-lighting	Apply colors for inserting, deleting, splitting, and merging of table cells.

Section	*Used To*
Formatting	Track formatting changes made to the content.
Balloons	Specify the formatting changes, insertions, deletions, and comments that need to be displayed in the balloon. It also allows you to specify the width of the balloon, align the balloon, and show or hide the lines connecting the balloon to the text.

How to Review a Document

Procedure Reference: Customize the Display of Track Changes

To customize the display of track changes:

1. Open a document.
2. On the Review tab, in the Tracking group, click the Track Changes drop-down arrow and choose Change Tracking Options.
3. In the Track Changes Options dialog box, specify the desired options.
4. Click OK.

Procedure Reference: Track Changes in a Document

To track changes in a document:

1. Enable track changes.
   - Right-click the Microsoft Office Status Bar and choose Track Changes to enable track changes using the Microsoft Office Status Bar.
   - Or, enable track changes using the Review tab.
     a. On the Ribbon, select the Review tab.
     b. On the Review tab, in the Tracking group, click Track Changes or click the Track Changes drop-down arrow and choose Track Changes.
2. If necessary, display the Word Options dialog box and update the user information.
3. Review the document and make changes, as necessary.
4. If necessary, disable track changes.
   - On the Review tab, in the Tracking group, click Track Changes.
   - Or, in the Microsoft Office Status Bar, choose Track Changes.

Procedure Reference: Insert a Comment

To insert a comment:

1. Select the location for the comment.
   - Select the text you want to comment on.
   - Or, place the insertion point where you want to insert a comment.
2. On the Review tab, in the Comments group, click New Comment to insert a comment.
3. Type the comment in the comment balloon.
4. If necessary, place the insertion point in the comment balloon and edit it.

Position the insertion point over any markup or comment balloon to display the reviewer's name.

5. If necessary, place the insertion point in the comment balloon.

6. Delete the comment balloon.

   ● On the Review tab, in the Comments group, click Delete.

   ● On the Review tab, in the Comments group, click the Delete drop-down arrow and select the desired option.

      ■ Select Delete to delete the comment where the insertion point is placed.

      ■ Select Delete All Comments Shown to delete the comments from a specific reviewer.

      ■ Or, select Delete All Comments In Document to delete all the comments in the document.

   ● Or, right-click a comment and choose Delete Comment.

ACTIVITY 2-3

Reviewing a Document

Data Files:

Milestones.docx

Before You Begin:

From the C:\084895Data\Collaborating on Documents folder, open Milestones.docx.

Scenario:

You have been included in the review cycle of Milestones.docx. Before you enable track changes and begin marking up the document, you decide to modify the track changes options to be consistent with the other reviewers. They use the following options:

- Insertions Color: Green
- Deletions Color: Red
- Comments: Turquoise
- Balloons: Only used for comments and formatting

What You Do	How You Do It
1. **Modify the options in the Markup and Balloons sections.**	a. On the Review tab, in the Tracking group, **click the Track Changes drop-down arrow and choose Change User Name.**
	b. If necessary, in the Personalize Your Copy Of Microsoft Office section, **type your first name, last name, and your initials and click OK.**
	c. In the Tracking group, **click the Track Changes drop-down arrow and choose Change Tracking Options.**
	d. In the Track Changes Options dialog box, in the Markup section, to the right of the Insertions drop-down list, from the Color drop-down list, **select Green.**
	e. Similarly, **select Red** to identify deletions.
	f. From the Comments drop-down list, **select Turquoise** to identify comments.
	g. In the Balloons section, in the Use Balloons (Print And Web Layout) drop-down list, **verify that the Only For Comments/Formatting option is selected and click OK.**
2. **Review the document.**	a. **Click the Track Changes drop-down arrow and choose Track Changes.**
	b. **Double-click the heading "Accomplishments" and type *Milestones***
	c. In the Comments group, **click New Comment.**
	d. In the comment balloon, **type *This heading should reflect the document's new name.***
	e. **Save the document as *My Milestones.docx* and close it.**

ACTIVITY 2-4

Modifying and Deleting Comments

Data Files:

Modified Milestones.docx

Before You Begin:

From the C:\084895Data\Collaborating on Documents folder, open Modified Milestones.docx.

Scenario:

You had reviewed a document and sent it to its author suggesting a few modifications. The author has sent it back to you for validation after making those changes.

What You Do	How You Do It
1. Delete the comments.	a. Place the insertion point at the end of the first comment. b. On the Review tab, in the Comments group, **click Delete.**
2. Modify the comment inserted for the second bullet point.	a. **Triple-click the comment inserted for the second bullet point.** b. **Type *I suggest you include the debt amount.*** c. **Save the document as *My Modified Milestones.docx* and close it.**

TOPIC D
Compare Document Changes

You tracked changes as you edited a document. However, when you have the original document and an edited copy, it can be difficult to identify subtle changes that have been made. In this topic, you will compare one document with another to clearly identify the changes between them.

You receive a copy of a document that you originally wrote. The person who gave you the copy did not enable the Track Changes option so you print the original and the copy and place them side by side on your desk, painstakingly comparing the two. Word provides a much more efficient method for comparing documents.

The Window Group

The Window group has a number of options that can be used for arranging, sizing, and managing multiple application windows.

The following table describes the options in the Window group.

Option	Description
New Window	Used to display a document in a new window.
Arrange All	Used to tile all the open windows horizontally.
Split	Used to split the window into multiple resizable panes to view different parts of a document.
View Side By Side	Used to view documents side-by-side for comparison.
Synchronous Scrolling	Used to synchronize the scrolling of documents that are displayed side-by-side.
Reset Window Position	Used to reset the window position of documents that are compared side-by-side by sharing the screen equally.
Switch Windows	Used to switch between open windows.

The Compare Documents Dialog Box

The Compare Documents dialog box enables users to compare two different versions of a document.

The following table describes the options in the Compare Documents dialog box.

Option	Description
Original Document drop-down list	Enables you to specify the name of the original document.
Revised Document drop-down list	Enables you to specify the name of the updated or revised document.

Option	Description
More button	Displays the advanced formatting options spread across two sections.
	• The Comparison Settings section: This section contains options for displaying or hiding the various changes that are made to documents.
	• Show Changes section: This section allows you to select where you want to view the compared changes—in the original, revised, or new document. You also have the option to observe the changes at the character or word level.

 Legal Blackline is a feature that compares two similar documents and displays the differences between them in a third document. Neither of the documents being compared is affected.

How to Compare Document Changes

Procedure Reference: Compare Documents

To compare documents:

1. Open the documents you want to compare.
2. On the View tab, in the Window group, click View Side By Side.
3. If necessary, in the Compare Side By Side dialog box, select the document to be compared.
4. If necessary, click Reset Window Position to position the windows side by side.
5. In either document, scroll up or down using the vertical scroll bar to browse the documents simultaneously and compare them.

 If the documents don't scroll together, on the View tab, in the Window group, click Synchronous Scrolling.

6. If necessary, make changes to the open documents.
7. If necessary, click View Side By Side to disable the option and display the documents separately.

Procedure Reference: Compare Document Changes

To compare document changes:

1. On the Review tab, in the Compare group, click Compare and choose Compare.
2. In the Compare Documents dialog box, select the original document.
   • From the Original Document drop-down list, select the desired document.
   • From the Original Document drop-down list, select Browse and navigate to and select the desired document.
   • Or, next to the Original Document drop-down list, click the Browse button and navigate to and select the desired document.

3. Select the revised document that you want to compare with the original document.

    ● From the Revised Document drop-down list, select the desired document.

    ● From the Revised Document drop-down list, select Browse and navigate to and select the desired document.

    ● Or, next to the Revised Document drop-down list, click the Browse button and navigate to and select the desired document.

4. If necessary, select the document in which the changes need to be displayed.

    a. Click More.

    b. In the Show Changes In section, select the desired option.

        ● Select Original Document to display the changes in the source document.

        ● Select Revised Document to display the changes in the edited document.

        ● Or, select New Document to display the changes in a new document.

5. Click OK to view the compared changes in the selected document.

ACTIVITY 2-5

Comparing Document Changes

Data Files:

Edited Milestones.docx, Edited Milestones Tm.docx

Before You Begin:

Open a blank document.

Scenario:

You sent the Edited Milestones document to Tim Mahoney for review and he has sent back his changes. Upon opening the document, you realize that he didn't enable track changes, so it isn't readily apparent what changes were made. You now need to figure out where he made changes without modifying either the original or the revised document.

What You Do	How You Do It
1. **Compare the original document with the revised one.**	a. On the Review tab, in the Compare group, **click Compare and choose Compare.**
	b. In the Compare Documents dialog box, from the Original Document drop-down list, **select Browse.**
	c. In the Open dialog box, **navigate to C:\ 084895Data\Collaborating on Documents, and open Edited Milestones.docx.**
	d. In the Compare Documents dialog box, from the Revised Document drop-down list, **select Browse.**
	e. In the Open dialog box, **double-click Edited Milestones Tm.docx and click More.**
	f. In the Show Changes section, **verify that the New Document option is selected by default and click OK.**
	g. Notice that the compared changes are highlighted in a new document.

2. **True or False? The new document with the compared changes opens in a new window.**

___ True

___ False

3. **Save and close the document.**

    a. **Save the compared document as *My Edited Milestones Tm.docx* and close it.**

    b. **Close all open documents.**

TOPIC E
Merge Document Changes

You have identified changes between two documents. Now, you may want to combine those changes into a single document. In this topic, you will merge changes from multiple documents.

You have several edited hard copies of your document in front of you. It would take several hours of uninterrupted work to enter all the changes in the original document. If the document changes had been made in electronic files rather than on paper, you could have quickly merged all of the document changes into one document, enabling you to begin your review of the changes immediately.

The Combine Documents Dialog Box

The Combine Documents dialog box enables the user to combine two different documents into one. The Original and the Revised drop-down lists allow you to specify the names of the original and revised documents, respectively. You can also set the comparison settings and choose whether you want the changes to be combined in the original.

How to Merge Document Changes

Procedure Reference: Merge Document Changes

To merge document changes:
1. On the Review tab, in the Compare group, click Compare and choose Combine.
2. In the Combine Documents dialog box, select the original document.
3. In the Combined Documents dialog box, select the document that contains the changes you want to combine with the original document.
4. If necessary, click More and, in the Show Changes In section, select an option based on the document in which the changes need to be displayed.
5. Click OK.

 If you wish to merge multiple copies into the current document, repeat the steps as needed.

ACTIVITY 2-6

Merging Document Changes

Data Files:

Edited Management Team.docx, Team Mc.docx, Team Sr.docx

Before You Begin:

Open a blank document.

Scenario:

You have received marked up copies of a document from multiple reviewers. You find it tedious to incorporate changes from one copy at a time.

What You Do	How You Do It
1. **Merge Team Mc.docx into Edited Management Team.docx.**	a. On the Review tab, in the Compare group, **click Compare and choose Combine.**
	b. In the Combine Documents dialog box, from the Original Document drop-down list, **select Browse.**
	c. In the Open dialog box, **navigate to C:\ 084895Data\Collaborating on Documents and double-click Edited Management Team.docx.**
	d. From the Revised Document drop-down list, **select Browse and double-click Team Mc.docx.**
	e. In the Show Changes section, **select the Original Document option and click OK.**
	f. **Save the combined document as *My Edited Management Team.docx***

2. **Merge Team Sr.docx into My Edited Management Team.docx.**

a. **Display the Combine Documents dialog box.**

b. In the Combine Documents dialog box, from the Original Document drop-down list, **select Browse and double-click My Edited Management Team.docx.**

c. From the Revised Document drop-down list, **select Browse and double-click Team Sr.docx.**

d. In the Show Changes section, **verify that the Original Document option is selected and click OK.**

e. Notice that the combined changes are displayed in the original My Edited Management Team document. **Save the document and close it.**

TOPIC F
Review Track Changes and Comments

You have merged all the tracked changes into a single document. Some of the changes are not necessary to create the desired final document. In this topic, you will accept and reject changes made to a document before sending out the final version.

Reviewing the tracked changes enables you to consider each suggestion or change and gives you the ability to accept or reject the suggested changes. This systematic approach also helps to ensure that you don't accidentally miss any markups no matter how small they are.

Full Screen Reading View

The purpose of Full Screen Reading view is to make documents easier to read and review on the screen. Full Screen Reading view enables you to increase or decrease the text's display size without actually affecting the document's text formatting. The pages are sized to enhance the reading experience without affecting the document's actual page setup.

View Options

The Full Screen Reading toolbar provides you with quick access to all the tools necessary to make it easier for you to read or review a document on screen. The View Options menu on the toolbar contains options relating to the display of pages and markup of a document. The following table describes the options available on the View Options menu.

Option	Used To
Don't Open Attachments In Full Screen	Restrict attachments opened from email applications and documents opened from the Sharepoint server from displaying in Full Screen Reading view.
Increase Text Size/Decrease Text Size	Increase or decrease the text size for easy reading.
Show One Page/Show Two Pages	Specify the number of pages to be displayed at one time.
Show Printed Page	Display the pages as they would look when printed. This option is similar to the Print Preview option accessible from the Microsoft Office button.
Margin Settings	Show, hide, or suppress margins on a printed page.
Allow Typing	Enable editing of the document while reading.
Track Changes	Enable track changes, specify the track change preferences, and change the reviewer's name and initials.
Show Comments And Changes	Select the type of markup to be displayed—comments, ink annotations, insertions and deletions, formatting, and markup area highlight. You can also choose to display changes and comments from specific reviewer(s).
Show Original/Final Document	Select whether you want to view the original or final document. You also have the option to view either of them with or without the changes.

The Navigation Pane

The Document Map or the Thumbnails pane is a navigation tool that appears in the left corner of a document and allows the user to quickly navigate to the desired location. The Document Map pane displays the headings and subheadings of the content in the document and the Thumbnails pane displays each page of the document as a small thumbnail.

How to Review Track Changes and Comments

Procedure Reference: Review Tracked Changes in Full Screen Reading View

To review tracked changes in Full Screen Reading view:

 If the document you want to review was sent to other mail recipients for review, you should click End Review on the Reviewing toolbar to indicate that the review stage has ended.

1. Switch to Full Screen Reading view.
    *   On the View tab, in the Document Views group, click Full Screen Reading.
    *   Or, in the Microsoft Office Status Bar, click the Full Screen Reading button.
2. Navigate to a particular section or page of the document using the Full Screen Reading toolbar.
    *   Click the Jump To A Page Or Section In The Document button, choose Document Map, and click the various headings to navigate through the document screens.
    *   Click the Jump To A Page Or Section In The Document button, choose Thumbnails, and click the various thumbnails to navigate through the document screens.
3. If necessary, position the mouse pointer over a marked up instance or a comment to identify the reviewer who is responsible for the change.
4. If necessary, show or hide comments from individual reviewers.
    a. Click View Options and choose Show Comments And Changes→Reviewers.
    b. Check a reviewer's name to show his or her comments, or uncheck reviewers whose comments you wish to hide.

Procedure Reference: Review Tracked Changes in Print Layout View

To review tracked changes in Print Layout view:

1. To display comments from a specific reviewer, on the Review tab, in the Tracking group, click Show Markup, choose Reviewers, and then select the desired reviewer from the list displayed.
2. Respond to a comment.
    a. Place the insertion point in the comment balloon.
    b. Insert a comment.

 Your comment will contain the letter "R" in the comment balloon where your initials are displayed, indicating that it is a response.

    c. Type your text in the comment balloon.

3. Accept or reject tracked changes and comments.

    a. If necessary, place the insertion point at the desired location in the document.

    b. On the Review tab, in the Changes group, click Previous or Next to move to the desired tracked change.

    c. Accept or reject the change.

    ● In the Changes group, click Accept to allow the insertion or deletion made to the document.

 When you accept a change that has a corresponding comment, you have the option of either retaining the comment by accepting it, or deleting it using the Reject button.

    ● Or, in the Changes group, click Reject to disallow the insertion or deletion made to the document.

 When you reject a change, both the change and the comment are deleted.

ACTIVITY 2-7

Reviewing Tracked Changes and Comments

Data Files:

Review Management Team.docx

Before You Begin:

From the C:\084895Data\Collaborating on Documents folder, open Review Management Team.docx.

Scenario:

With all the changes merged into the Review Management Team document, you now need to review the changes and accept or reject them, as needed.

What You Do	How You Do It
1. **Preview the document changes in Full Screen Reading view.**	a. In the Microsoft Office Status Bar, **click the Full Screen Reading button,** to switch to Full Screen Reading view.
	b. On the toolbar, **click the Jump To A Page Or Section In The Document button and choose Document Map.**
	c. In the Document Map pane, observe the green headings that indicate inserted text. **Click Talent** to display the relevant content on page four.
	d. In the Document Map pane, **click Management Team** to return to the beginning of the document.
	e. On the Full Screen Reading toolbar, **click the Jump To A Page Or Section In The Document button and choose Thumbnails.**
	f. In the Thumbnails pane, observe that the comment balloons and markups are visible, but not legible. **Verify that the first thumbnail is selected.**

> Both the Document Map and Thumbnails show document markups.

2. Review the changes.

    a. At the top-right corner of the window, **click Close** to close the full screen view.

    b. On the Review tab, in the Changes group, **click Next.**

    c. Notice that the word "subsequent" was deleted. In the Changes group, **click Accept.**

    d. Notice that the word "prior" was inserted. **Click Accept** to accept the change.

    e. Observe that the Relocation Services paragraph is highlighted. In the Changes group, **click Reject.**

    f. Notice that both the inserted text and the comment have been deleted. **Click Next** to move to the next change.

    g. **Accept the deletion of the name Joan.**

    h. **Accept the insertion of the name John.**

    i. Notice that the comment is highlighted. **Click Reject** to delete the comment.

    j. **Accept the insertion of ", Accounting."**

    k. **Delete Mary's comment.**

    l. **Reject the Today's Opportunities insertion made by Todd.**

---

3. Respond to Justin Altman's comment.

    a. **Click in the Justin Altman's comment** and, in the Comments group, **click New Comment.**

    b. Observe that a new comment balloon is displayed with an 'R' after your user name to indicate it is a response. **Type *Names have been confirmed.***

> **Comment [JA1]:** Can someone please confirm the names of these new hires?
>
> **Comment [JA2R1]:** Names have been confirmed.

    c. **Save the document as *My Review Management Team.docx* and close it.**

Lesson 2 Follow-up

In this lesson, you collaborated on several documents. You input your user information to help identify the changes you made, sent a document for review, and tracked changes as you edited a document. You then compared and merged document changes before reviewing the tracked changes and accepting and rejecting those changes, as needed. Collaborating on a document in Word makes edits more readable and easy to incorporate.

1. **How will you use Word to collaborate on documents at your office?**

2. **What types of documents are you asked to collaborate on in your daily work?**

3 | Managing Document Versions

Lesson Time: 1 hour(s)

Lesson Objectives:

In this lesson, you will manage document versions.

You will:

● Create a new version of a document.

● Compare document versions.

● Merge document versions.

Introduction

You know how to collaborate on documents. When a document goes through the collaboration process, multiple versions of the document are created. In this topic, you will manage document versions.

Your document may go through many rounds of reviews, which could result in the creation of multiple document versions. Managing the different document versions could be made easier if there was a central repository for the documents created.

TOPIC A
Create a New Version of a Document

There may be times when you want to save changes to a document without overwriting it. You could save the modified document with a different file name, but if you need to retain changes to many documents, this could cause confusion. In this topic, you will create new versions of a document.

Your manager reviews the annual report you wrote. It is a little long, so she asks you to remove all data tables and charts. After another review, she decides that the report was better with the tables and charts and wants you to put them all back in. Since a version of the document with the tables and charts was saved, you simply send the earlier version to your manager, saving yourself a day or more of work.

Microsoft® Office SharePoint® Server 2007

Microsoft® Office SharePoint® Server 2007 is a collaboration and content management server that is integrated with the Office 2007 suite. It acts as a repository to save documents from across different locations. It can also be used to control access and content modification permissions to these documents. It tracks the work done on a document by maintaining information on the users and document versions. The SharePoint server acts as a common platform for hosting content from the Internet or an intranet.

Versioning

Versioning is the process of recording and storing changes made to a document over the course of its development. Each time the document is checked in to the server, changes made since the previous version are stored in the latest version of the document. As the file accumulates versions, you have the ability to revisit, review, and reuse each of these versions.

How to Create a New Version of a Document

Procedure Reference: Create a Document Workspace from Microsoft® Office Word 2007

To create a document workspace from Microsoft Office Word 2007:

1. Open the document you want to upload to a SharePoint site.
2. Click the Office button and choose Publish→Create Document Workspace.
3. In the Document Management pane, triple-click in the Document Workspace Name text box and type a name for the document workspace.
4. Specify the location on the SharePoint server where you want to create your workspace.
    *   Click in the Location For New Workspace text box and type the URL to the SharePoint server.
    *   Or, from the Location For New Workspace drop-down list, select an existing SharePoint server.
5. Click Create to create a new workspace and save the document in it.
6. If necessary, in the Document Management pane, click Open Site In Browser to open the workspace in Internet Explorer.

Procedure Reference: Specify Versioning Settings in a SharePoint Site

To specify versioning settings in a SharePoint site:

1. On the home page of the document workspace, in the right pane, click the Shared Documents link.

2. On the Shared Documents page, click Settings and choose Document Library Settings.

3. On the Customize Shared Documents page, under the General Settings section, click Versioning Settings.

4. On the Document Library Versioning Settings: Shared Documents page, specify the appropriate versioning settings.

5. Click OK.

Versioning Settings

The Document Library Versioning Settings: Shared Documents page provides you with options that help control the versioning of the documents you want to share using the SharePoint server.

Section	Allows You To
Content Approval	Specify if the edited content of a document requires approval before it is saved as a version.
Document Version History	Enable and disable versioning. If enabled, you can specify whether you want to create a major version for every edited document or save a version as draft—a minor version—until the edited content is approved. You can also specify the number of versions you want to retain for a document.
Draft Item Security	Control who can view the draft copies of a document.
Require Check Out	Specify whether documents must be checked out before they can be edited. If the option is set to Yes, then unless checked out, a document opens in read-only mode.

Procedure Reference: Access Documents in a SharePoint Server

To access documents in a SharePoint server:

1. Check out a document.

   ● Check out the document using the SharePoint server.

     a. On the home page of the workspace, under Shared Documents, place the mouse pointer over the document you want to check out, and from the menu that is displayed, choose Check Out.

> If you have just checked in the document, you may have to refresh the web page to update the menu options.

     b. In the message box that indicates that you are about to check out the specified document, click OK.

    c.   In the Shared Documents section, notice that a green box with an arrow appears near the Word 2007 file icon to indicate that the document has been checked out. If necessary, navigate to the location where the checked-out files are saved and open the document.

 Use the options in the Save category of the Word Options dialog box to specify where you want to save the checked-out files from your document management server. By default, files are saved to the SharePoint Drafts folder in My Documents.

- Check out the document using Word 2007.

    a.   Open a document that is to be checked out from the SharePoint site.

    b.   Click the Office button and choose Server→Check Out.

    c.   In the Edit Offline message box that indicates the location where your checked-out copy will be stored, click OK.

    d.   If necessary, navigate to the location where your checked-out files are saved, and open the document.

2.   If necessary, view the version history.

    a.   Click the Office button and choose Server→View Version History to display the different versions of the document available in the Versions Saved For [File Name] dialog box.

    b.   Select an option in order to work with the different versions displayed.

- In the Comments column, click a comment to view it completely in the Check In Comments message box and then click Close.

- Select a version and click Open to view that version of the document.

- Select a version and click Compare to compare the selected version with the current version.

- Select a version and click Restore to replace the current version of the document with the earlier version.

- Or, select a version and click Delete to delete it.

    c.   Click Close to close the dialog box.

3.   If necessary, make the desired changes to the document.

4.   Check in the document.

- Check in the document using the SharePoint server.

    a.   On the home page of the workspace, under Shared Documents, place the mouse pointer over the document you want to check in, and from the menu that is displayed, choose Check In.

    b.   If necessary, on the Check In page, in the Comments text area, type your comments.

    c.   Click OK.

- Check in the document using Word 2007.

    a.   Click the Office button and choose Server→Check In.

    b.   If necessary, in the Check In dialog box, in the Version Comments text area, type your comments on the changes made to the version.

c.   Click OK.

Accessing Documents Directly from a SharePoint Site

Documents that are already saved in a SharePoint site can also be accessed by browsing to the
SharePoint site. You can enter the URL to the workspace directly in Internet Explorer. You can
then check out, check in, and view the different versions of a document as you can in Word
2007.

DISCOVERY ACTIVITY 3-1
Creating a New Version of a Document

Data Files:

Creating a New Version_guided.exe

Setup:

This is a simulated activity. In this simulation, SharePoint Server 2007 has been installed with the following URL: http://adexchangesrv:34097.

Scenario:

Your company has decided to use SharePoint 2007 as its content management server. Since you are part of the team developing content, your machine has been configured to the server and you are expected to start using it for your next project, which is the company's annual report. You have just completed the first draft and sent it to your manager. After a quick review, your manager asks you to change the increase in the net income, portfolio, and capitalization values in the Milestones section. You are doubtful about the changes, but because you are unable to clarify them right away, you decide to incorporate them anyway. You want to be able to access the original version in case you need it later.

1. To launch the simulation, **browse to the C:\084895Data\Managing Document Versions\ Simulations folder.**

2. **Double-click the Creating a New Version_guided.exe file.**

3. **Maximize the simulation window.**

4. **Follow the on-screen steps for the simulation.**

5. When you have finished the activity, **close the simulation window.**

TOPIC B
Compare Document Versions

You have created versions of a document. You now need to identify the changes made to the latest version of the document in relation to the original document. In this topic, you will compare document versions.

The editor reviewing your document asks you to change the heading and the introduction paragraph. You make the changes she indicated and send it back for her verification. She responds, saying that the introduction paragraph in the earlier version of the document related better to the heading in the latest version of the document. With the help of Word, you can easily compare the two versions of a document and identify the changes made.

How to Compare Document Versions
Procedure Reference: Compare Two Versions of a Document

To compare two versions of a document:

1. Check out a version of the document you want to compare.
2. On the Review tab, click Compare and choose the version type you want to use for comparison to open both the new document with the tracked changes and the selected version of the document, simultaneously.

   - Choose Major Version to compare the document to its last major version.
   - Choose Last Version to compare the document to the last major or minor version, whichever applicable, of the document.
   - Choose Specific Version and, in the Versions Saved For [File Name] dialog box, select the desired version.

 These options will be listed in the Compare option only if the versioning settings for the document are turned on in the SharePoint site.

DISCOVERY ACTIVITY 3-2
Comparing Two Versions of a Document

Data Files:

Comparing Versions_guided.exe

Setup:

This is a simulated activity. In this simulation, a SharePoint site has been created for your team with a document library.

Scenario:

After you made the changes to the report based on your manager's suggestions, you get a call from him stating that he was wrong about the portfolio and capitalization values and would like for you to retain their original values. Since the review, you have been working on other reports and you do not recall all the changes you made to the annual report.

1. To launch the simulation, **browse to the C:\084895Data\Managing Document Versions\ Simulations folder.**

2. **Double-click the Comparing Versions_guided.exe file.**

3. **Maximize the simulation window.**

4. **Follow the on-screen steps for the simulation.**

5. When you have finished the activity, **close the simulation window.**

TOPIC C
Merge Document Versions

In the previous topic, you compared versions of a document. After having identified the changes made in different versions of the document, you may now need to combine them into a single document so that you can review them. In this topic, you will merge document versions.

You have your document back from multiple rounds of reviews. You realize that you received a number of edits from all the reviewers with respect to your language. You would like to take a look at the feedback suggested by all the reviewers.

How to Merge Document Versions

Procedure Reference: Merge Multiple Versions of a Document

To merge multiple versions of a document:

1. Check out the latest version of the document from the SharePoint site.
2. Open the document versions that you want to merge.
   a. Click the Office button and choose Server→View Version History.
   b. Select the version you want to open.
   c. Click Open.
3. Display the Combine Documents dialog box.
4. From the Original Document drop-down list, select a version.

 To display a version as an option in the Original Document and Revised Document drop-down lists, you must first open the version of the document using the Versions Saved For [File Name] dialog box.

5. From the Revised Document drop-down list, select the version you want to combine with the original document.
6. If necessary, click More, and in the Show Changes In section, select the option based on the document in which the combined changes need to be displayed.
7. Click OK.

 If the Microsoft Office Word dialog box appears, select the document for which you want to retain the formatting changes.

DISCOVERY ACTIVITY 3-3
Merging Multiple Versions of a Document

Data Files:

Merging Versions_guided.exe

Setup:

This is a simulated activity. In this simulation, a SharePoint site has been created for your team with a document library.

Scenario:

As a new employee, the annual report is the first official document you have been asked to work on. You would like to study the changes suggested by the different reviewers in the previous versions of the report so that you can create a report that meets their requirements. However, there is a different version in SharePoint for each reviewer and looking up each version can be tedious.

1. To launch the simulation, **browse to the C:\084895Data\Managing Document Versions\ Simulations folder.**

2. **Double-click the Merging Versions_guided.exe file.**

3. **Maximize the simulation window.**

4. **Follow the on-screen steps for the simulation.**

5. When you have finished the activity, **close the simulation window.**

Lesson 3 Follow-up

In this lesson, you managed the different versions of a document that are created automatically each time a document is checked into SharePoint Server 2007.

1. **In your daily work, do you find it useful to compare different document versions? Why?**

2. **How beneficial is SharePoint Server 2007 when collaborating with documents at your workplace?**

4 | Adding Reference Marks and Notes

Lesson Time: 1 hour(s)

Lesson Objectives:

In this lesson, you will add reference marks and notes.

You will:

- Insert bookmarks.
- Insert footnotes and endnotes.
- Add captions to illustrations.
- Add hyperlinks.
- Add cross-references.
- Add citations and a bibliography.

Introduction

You managed multiple versions of a document. When working with large documents, being able to mark specific locations and provide additional descriptive information can make them easier to use. In this lesson, you will use various techniques to add reference marks and notes.

While working with large documents, it is always handy to include information on sources of content alongside the document content. Apart from enabling you to keep track of the source, using these references helps your readers gain knowledge about interesting facts or other nice-to-know information regarding the content, without diverting their attention from the main document.

TOPIC A
Insert Bookmarks

You have completed work on your document. Now, you may need to create references that make browsing through the document easier. In this topic, you will insert bookmarks.

As you are checking a long document for accuracy, you come across a fact that you are unsure of. Since you want to keep going, you insert a bookmark. That way, when you have time, you can return directly to the fact in question rather than waste time scrolling through the entire document trying to find your place.

Bookmarks

Bookmarks are markers within a document that enable users to quickly return to a given location. They can be used to mark important information or interesting facts in the document. In Microsoft® Office Word 2007, you can access the Bookmark option from the Links group on the Insert tab.

Other Uses of Bookmarks

Apart from using bookmarks to mark and locate important information in the document, you can use bookmarks for other purposes. You can insert a cross-reference to a bookmark's text, page number, and paragraph number. Also, you can insert a bookmarked portion of another document into the current document.

Bookmark Formatting Marks

When you insert a bookmark into a document, the bookmarked location is marked by the bookmark formatting mark. This mark can be displayed using the options in the Word Options dialog box. The bookmark formatting marks that appear vary based on the content being bookmarked. For instance, when you insert a bookmark for a specific location, the bookmark formatting mark is displayed as an I-beam. It appears as brackets when inserted for a selection.

The Bookmark Dialog Box

The Bookmark dialog box contains options that enable you to add, delete, or navigate to a bookmark in a document. In the Sort By section, you can choose to sort the list of available bookmarks either by name or by location. You also have the option to display a list of hidden bookmarks in the Bookmark Name list box.

> Hidden bookmarks are generally created by Word to mark certain fields in the document. They can also be created using Visual Basic for Applications (VBA), Visual Basic (VB), or other automation languages. These bookmarks are not indicated by bookmark formatting marks.

Handwritten margin note: Establish levels in your document to navigate easier to navigate throughout the document.

How to Insert Bookmarks

Procedure Reference: Insert Bookmarks

To insert bookmarks:

1. If necessary, display bookmark formatting marks.

    a. Open the Word Options dialog box.

    b. In the Advanced category, in the Show Document Content section, check the Show Bookmarks check box.

    c. Click OK to close the Word Options dialog box.

2. Select the location, section, or item where you want to insert the bookmark.

3. Display the Bookmark dialog box.

    *   On the Insert tab, in the Links group, click Bookmark.

    *   Or, press Ctrl+Shift+F5.

4. In the Bookmark Name text box, type a name for the bookmark.

 While naming a bookmark, do not include spaces between words. Instead, use an underscore to indicate a space. For example, my_bookmark.

5. Click Add to insert the new bookmark.

6. If necessary, navigate to a bookmark.

    a. Display the Bookmark dialog box.

    b. Select a bookmark and click Go To.

7. If necessary, in the Bookmark dialog box, select the bookmark and click Delete to delete a bookmark.

8. Close the Bookmark dialog box.

Procedure Reference: Insert a Bookmarked Portion of Another Document into the Current Document

To insert a bookmarked portion of another document into the current document:

1. If necessary, open the document that includes the bookmarked content you want to copy and the document to which you want to copy the bookmarked content.

2. Place the insertion point in a blank line after the text where you wish to include the Bookmarked content.

3. On the Insert tab, in the Text group, click the Object drop-down arrow and choose Text From File.

4. In the Insert File dialog box, navigate to the file that contains the bookmarked content and click Range.

5. In the Set Range dialog box, type the name of the bookmark you wish to insert and click OK.

6. In the Insert File dialog box, click Insert.

ACTIVITY 4-1

Using Bookmarks

Data Files:

Annual Report.docx

Before You Begin:

From the C:\084895Data\Adding Reference Marks and Notes folder, open Annual Report.docx.

Scenario:

You are working on the annual financial report of the company. As you glance through your document, you realize that the content on page 10 is important and you may need to refer to this page several times. You want an easy method for navigating to that content rather than scrolling through the pages. You also find that the title "Financial Overview" has been bookmarked. Since you do not find the content important, you decide to remove the bookmark to keep your document neat and organized.

What You Do	How You Do It
1. **Bookmark the title "Talent" on page 11.**	a. **Display the Advanced category in the Word Options dialog box.**
	b. In the Show Document Content section, **check the Show Bookmarks check box.**
	c. **Click OK** to close the Word Options dialog box and display the bookmark formatting marks.
	d. In the Document Map pane, **click Talent.**
	e. On the Insert tab, in the Links group, **click Bookmark.**
	f. In the Bookmark dialog box, in the Bookmark Name text box, **type *Talent***
	g. **Click Add.**
	h. Notice that an I-beam is displayed near the text "Talent" indicating the presence of a bookmark.

2. **Bookmark the paragraph on "Strategy" on page 4 along with the graphic in it.**

   a. In the Document Map pane, **click "Strategy"** to display page 4.

   b. **Select the "Strategy" paragraph along with the graphic below it.**

   c. **Press Ctrl+Shift+F5.**

   d. In the Bookmark dialog box, in the Bookmark Name text box, **type *Strategy* and click Add.**

   e. **Click off the graphic** to deselect it.

   f. Notice that the title "Strategy" and the graphic below are enclosed in brackets.

3. **Delete the "Finance" bookmark.**

   a. **Display the Bookmark dialog box.**

   b. In the Bookmark Name list box, **select Finance and click Go To.**

   c. **Click Delete.**

   d. **Click Close** to close the Bookmark dialog box.

   e. Notice that the bookmark formatting mark before the "Financial Overview" title has been removed, indicating that the bookmark has been deleted.

   f. **Save the file as *My Annual Report.docx***

TOPIC B
Insert Footnotes and Endnotes

You have inserted bookmarks for quick reference to specific content. In the course of your work, you may have referenced or reused thoughts or ideas presented by other authors. In this topic, you will insert footnotes and endnotes citing references to borrowed content.

As you are writing an article for a trade journal, you come across published research that supports your article's premise. Therefore, you use some of the research in your article, but neglect to credit the source. Whether you intended to, you just took credit for someone else's work. You could find yourself in serious legal trouble if you use someone else's work without giving them credit. Properly citing the research in a footnote or an endnote can help you avoid this situation.

Footnotes and Endnotes

A *footnote* is a note that is inserted at the bottom of a page. It is associated with a particular term in the document and is used to provide additional information about that term or to cite references to the source of the term. It is always added to the same page as the text that is marked. *Endnotes* are similar to footnotes, except that they are inserted at the end of a section. The note reference mark that appears both after the relevant term and before the footnote or endnote indicates the connection between them.

The Footnote And Endnote Dialog Box

The Footnote And Endnote dialog box contains three sections, each with options to add, format, and modify a footnote or an endnote.

The following table describes the options available in the Footnote And Endnote dialog box.

Option	Description
Footnotes or Endnotes	Enables users to insert a footnote or an endnote in the document. Selecting either option enables the corresponding drop-down list, where the user can select the location of the note.
Convert	Displays the Convert Notes dialog box. This dialog box provides users with options that help to convert all footnotes to endnotes, all endnotes to footnotes, or to swap the footnotes and endnotes of the document.
Number Format	Provides options that help to format the numbers or symbols that represent the footnote or the endnote. The available formats include asterisks , roman numerals, and alphabets.
Custom Mark	Enables the user to insert a default numbering format for the note type selected. Inserting a custom mark will disable other formatting options.
Symbol	Displays the Symbol dialog box. The user can choose any symbol to use it as a custom mark.
Start At	Provides options that help to format the number or symbol that represents the first footnote or the endnote in a document.

Option	Description
Numbering	Enables users to specify whether the numbering of the reference notes should be continuous, restart at the end of every section, or restart at the end of every page.
Apply Changes To	Enables users to apply the specified format to a specific section or to the whole document.

How to Insert Footnotes and Endnotes

Procedure Reference: Insert a Footnote or an Endnote

To insert a footnote or an endnote:

1. Place the insertion point where you want the note's reference mark to be inserted.
2. Add a note.
   - Use the Footnote And Endnote dialog box.
     a. On the References tab, in the Footnotes group, click the Dialog Box Launcher button.
     b. In the Footnote And Endnote dialog box, select the Footnotes or Endnotes option and click Insert.
   - Use the Footnotes group on the References tab.
     - Click Insert Footnote to insert a footnote.
     - Click Insert Endnote to insert an endnote.
   - Or, use shortcut keys.
     - Press Ctrl+Alt+F insert a footnote.
     - Press Ctrl+Alt+D to insert an endnote.
3. If necessary, select the note and press Delete to delete the note.

Procedure Reference: Modify a Footnote or an Endnote

To modify a footnote or an endnote:

1. Display the Footnote And Endnote dialog box.
   - On the References tab, in the Footnotes group, click the Dialog Box Launcher button.
   - Or, right-click the footnote or endnote and choose Note Options.
2. Modify the note, as desired.
   - Modify the location of the note.
     - Select the Footnotes option, and from the drop-down list, select Bottom Of Page or Below Text.
     - Or, select the Endnotes option, and from the drop-down list, select End Of Section or End Of Document.
   - If necessary, convert a note from one type to another.
     a. In the Location section, click Convert.
     b. In the Convert Notes dialog box, select the desired option.

    c.   Click OK.

● Modify the reference mark's format options.

    ■   From the Number Format drop-down list, select a number format.

    ■   In the Custom Mark text box, enter a symbol.

    ■   In the Start At spin box, click the up or down arrow to determine the Start At number or symbol, or type in the spin box.

    ■   Or, from the Numbering drop-down list, determine whether the numbering will be Continuous, Restart Each Section, or Restart Each Page.

3. If necessary, from the Apply Changes To drop-down list, determine whether to apply changes to either the selected text or to the document as a whole.

4. Click Insert.

Tooltips for Footnotes and Endnotes

You do not have to navigate to the note area to read an endnote or a footnote. Just by placing the insertion point over the note's reference mark, you can view a tooltip containing the note text.

ACTIVITY 4-2

Inserting Footnotes and Endnotes

Before You Begin:

My Annual Report.docx is open.

Scenario:

You are working on the annual financial report. The report's lead editor has asked you to clarify two points. She wants you to footnote the sources of the data used in the Residential section's chart and table. She has also requested that you add notes explaining why the team was created. To meet company style guidelines, the notes should go at the end of the text's section rather than the end of the document.

What You Do	How You Do It
1. Insert a footnote explaining the source of the chart and table data.	a. In the Document Map pane, **click "Residential"**.
	b. **Place the insertion point at the end of the "Residential" paragraph.**
	c. On the References tab, in the Footnotes group, **click Insert Footnote.**
	d. **Type *The chart and table data are from the Census Bureau's June 2003 New Residential Sales press release.***

2. **Insert an uppercase Roman numeral endnote at the end of the New Relocation Team section.**

a. In the Document Map pane, **click New Relocation Team.**

b. **Place the insertion point at the end of the "New Relocation Team" paragraph.**

c. In the Footnotes group, **click the Dialog Box Launcher button** to display the Footnote And Endnote dialog box.

d. In the Location section, **select the Endnotes option.**

e. From the Endnotes drop-down list, **select End Of Section.**

f. In the Format section, from the Number Format drop-down list, **select I, II, III.**

g. In the Apply Changes section, in the Apply Changes To drop-down list, **verify that This Section is selected.**

h. **Click Insert.**

i. In the note area, **type *The new team was created to take advantage of current and near-term market trends.***

j. **Right-click in the endnote area and choose Go To Endnote** to navigate to the note's reference mark in the text.

TOPIC C
Add Captions

You have inserted footnotes and endnotes in your document. Apart from these references, you may also want to number and add descriptive information to accompany equations, figures, or tables in the document. In this topic, you will add captions.

In textbooks, manuals, and other large documents, objects such as equations, figures, and tables are usually numbered and have a brief description so that they can be easily referred to in the text. You can manually type your own captions, but you can use Word to automatically number captions of equations, figures, or tables without having to manually keep track of the numbering.

Captions

Definition:

A *caption* is a phrase that describes an object such as a picture, graphic, equation, or table. It identifies the relevance of an object to the content. A caption can be placed above or below the object. In Word, captions can be inserted by using the Insert Caption option in the Captions group of the References tab.

Example:

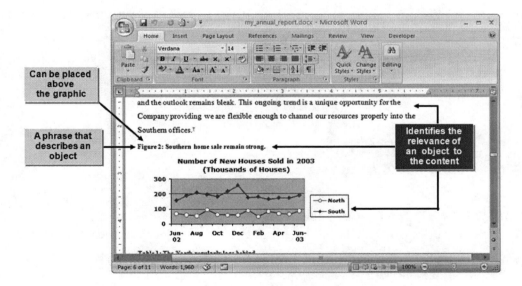

The Caption Dialog Box

The Caption dialog box provides options that enable a user to add or format a caption.

The following table describes the options available in the Caption dialog box.

Option	Description
Caption	Enables users to type the caption text. This text box displays the caption title based on the label and numbering format.
Label	Enables users to select the type of caption, such as tables, figures, or equations, to be added to the object.
Position	Enables users to position the caption above or below the selected object.
Exclude Label From Caption	Removes the label affixed to the caption title.
New Label	Displays the New Label dialog box, which enables users to specify a new label.
Delete Label	Enables users to delete a label. This option is active only after a new label is created.
Numbering	Displays the Caption Numbering dialog box with options for formatting the numbering of the caption.
AutoCaption	Displays the AutoCaption dialog box. This dialog box contains options that enable Word to automatically add captions to objects in a document.

Updating Fields

When you use the AutoCaption option, Word may not automatically update all the caption numbers. To update all the caption numbers and other fields in the document simultaneously, select the entire document and press F9. To update the numbering of a single caption, right-click the caption and choose Update Field.

How to Add Captions

Procedure Reference: Add a Caption

To add a caption:

1. Browse to the object to which you want to add a caption.

   a. Click the Select Browse Object button and choose the object you want to browse by.

   b. Click either the Previous [object] button or the Next [object] button to navigate to the last or next instance of the selected object.

2. Display the Caption dialog box.

   - On the References tab, in the Captions group, click Insert Caption.

   - Or, right-click the selected object and choose Insert Caption.

3. In the Caption text box, type the description for the object.

4. In the Caption dialog box, in the Options section, from the Label drop-down list, select the type of caption you wish to insert.

5. If necessary, using the options in the Position drop-down list, position the caption below or above the object.

6. Click OK to insert the caption.

7. If necessary, modify the caption.

    a. Display the Caption dialog box.

    b. Specify the desired settings.

    - Click New Label, and in the New Label dialog box, type the name of the label and click OK.

    - Click Numbering, and in the Caption Numbering dialog box, set the format of the caption number and click OK.

    c. Click OK.

ACTIVITY 4-3

Adding Captions

Before You Begin:

My Annual Report.docx is open.

Close the Document Map pane.

Scenario:

You have been asked to create an annual report with supporting objects such as graphics, photographs, and financial charts. You want to make these objects in the annual report easier for people to understand and relate to.

What You Do	How You Do It
1. Add a descriptive figure caption above the Relocation team's organization chart.	a. **Select the organization chart on page 8.**
	b. On the References tab, in the Captions group, **click Insert Caption.**
	c. In the Caption dialog box, in the Caption text box, **type** *: The Relocation management team.*
	d. In the Options section, in the Label drop-down list, **verify that Figure is selected.**
	e. From the Position drop-down list, **select Above Selected Item and click OK.**

2. **Add a descriptive figure caption above the House Sale graphic.**

    a. Near the bottom of the scroll bar, **click the Select Browse Object button and choose Browse By Graphic.**

    b. **Click the Previous Graphic button and select the Number Of New Houses Sold chart.**

    c. **Display the Caption dialog box.**

    d. In the Caption text box, **type** *: Southern home sales remain strong.*

    e. **Verify that Figure is selected in the Label drop-down list box.**

    f. **Verify that Above Selected Item is selected in the Position drop-down list box. Click OK.**

    g. Similarly, on page 4, **add a caption that reads** *: Teamwork is critical to our success.* to the teamwork graphic.

3. **Add a descriptive table caption above the New Houses Sold table.**

    a. **Click the Select Browse Object button and choose Browse By Table.**

    b. **Display the Caption dialog box.**

    c. In the Caption text box, **type** *: The North regularly lags behind.*

    d. In the Options section, from the Label drop-down list, **select Table and click OK.**

    e. **Save the document and close it.**

TOPIC D
Add Hyperlinks

You have added numbers and descriptive information to illustrations in your document to help associate the illustrations with the related content. Now, you may want to provide a means by which users can easily navigate to related content both within and outside of the document. In this topic, you will insert hyperlinks.

Your manager has nominated you to represent the organization at a seminar. She wants you to give a presentation that includes a detailed report on each product to provide to interested audience members. Rather than providing textual references in the presentation to each related report, you can use hyperlinks to enable users to navigate to the desired report.

Hyperlinks

Definition:

A *hyperlink* is a navigation tool that links content in a document to related information, thereby enabling the user to directly navigate to the information. The link is always represented by highlighted words or images. A hyperlink can be inserted for a document, web page, text, figure, or table.

Example:

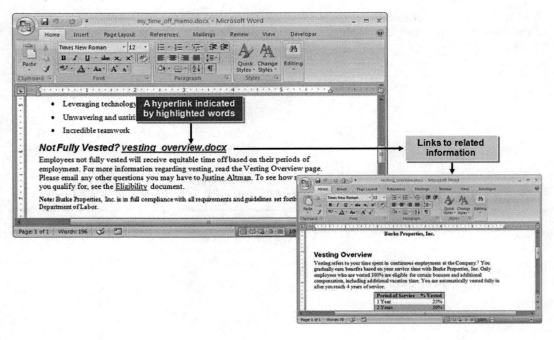

The Insert Hyperlink Dialog Box

The options in the Insert Hyperlink dialog box enable the user to insert a hyperlink to a new document, preexisting document, a web page or to an email address.

Section	Description
Link To	Contains options that help to link the current document to an existing file, a web page, content in the same document, a new document, or an email address.
Text To Display	Enables the user to enter text that is to be displayed as the hyperlink. The user can also insert a ScreenTip that will be displayed when the reader moves the mouse pointer over the hyperlink.
Look In	Contains options that help to navigate to and link a document or web page to the current document. The name and the options in this section vary based on the option selected in the Link To section.

Options in the Look In Section

The section below the Text To Display section changes based on the option selected in the Link To section.

Option Selected in the Link To Section	Section Below the Text To Display Section
Existing File Or Web Page	Displays the Look In section. The various options in this section enable the user to link to an already existing document or web page.
Place In This Document	Displays the Select A Place In This Document section. The Select A Place In This Document list box enables the user to link to a particular location in the current document.
Create New Document	Displays the Name Of New Document section. The options in this section enable the user to link to a new document.
E-mail Address	Displays the E-Mail Address section. The options in this section enable the user to link to an email address. Clicking the link to the email address displays the Message tab in Microsoft® Office Outlook®.

How to Add Hyperlinks

Procedure Reference: Insert a Hyperlink

To insert a hyperlink to a document:

1. Place the insertion point where you wish to insert the hyperlink or select the text you want to use as a hyperlink.

2. Display the Hyperlink dialog box.

    *   On the Insert tab, in the Links group, click Hyperlink.
    *   Press Ctrl+K.
    *   Or, right-click the selected text and choose Hyperlink.

3. In the Text To Display text box, type the text that is to be displayed as the hyperlink. If you have selected the text, it is displayed by default and can be modified, if desired.

4. If necessary, add a ScreenTip.

    a. Click ScreenTip.
    b. In the Set Hyperlink Screen Tip dialog box, type the ScreenTip that you want to display.
    c. Click OK.

5. In the Link To section, select the Existing File Or Web Page option.

6. In the Look In section, select the file to be linked to.

7. Click OK.

8. If necessary, Ctrl-click or right-click the hyperlink and choose Open Hyperlink to navigate to the linked text or content.

9. If necessary, right-click the hyperlink, choose Edit Hyperlink, make the necessary changes, and click OK to modify the hyperlink.

10. If necessary, delete a hyperlink.

    *   Delete the hyperlink using the Edit Source dialog box.
        a. Right-click the link and choose Edit Hyperlink.
        b. In the Edit Hyperlink dialog box, click Remove Link.
    *   Or, select the hyperlink and press Delete.

The Edit Hyperlink Dialog Box

The Edit Hyperlink dialog box contains options that help to modify or edit the hyperlink. The options in the Edit Hyperlink dialog box are similar to the options in the Insert Hyperlink dialog box. However, this dialog box provides an additional option for deleting the selected link.

ACTIVITY 4-4

Inserting Hyperlinks

Data Files:

Time Off Memo.docx, Eligibility.docx, Vesting Overview.docx

Before You Begin:

From the C:\084895Data\Adding Reference Marks and Notes folder, open Time Off Memo.docx.

Scenario:

As the HR executive of your firm, you have been assigned the task of composing a memo to inform the employees of the number of days off they are allowed. Right now, the details pertaining to the different types of employee time-off are available in different documents. You need to include all the information in these documents in your memo without making it look cluttered.

What You Do	How You Do It
1. **Link the Vesting Overview.docx file to the "Not Fully Vested?" paragraph.**	a. **Place the insertion point after the title "Not Fully Vested?" and press the Spacebar.**
	b. On the Insert tab, in the Links group, **click Hyperlink.**
	c. In the Insert Hyperlink dialog box, **click ScreenTip.**
	d. In the Set Hyperlink ScreenTip dialog box, **type _Click here to display the Vesting Overview.docx file._ and click OK.**
	e. In the Link To section, **verify that Existing File Or Web Page is selected.**
	f. In the Look In list box, **select the Vesting Overview.docx file and click OK.**
	g. Notice that the hyperlink is highlighted in blue to distinguish it from the rest of the text. **Place the mouse pointer over the Vesting Overview hyperlink** to view the ScreenTip.
	h. **Ctrl-click** to open the Vesting Overview.docx file.
	i. **Close the Vesting Overview.docx file.**
2. **Link the word "Eligibility" to the Eligibility.docx file.**	a. In the first paragraph below the title "Not Fully Vested?", in the last line, **right-click the word "Eligibility" and choose Hyperlink.**
	b. **Insert a ScreenTip that reads _Click here to open the Eligibility document._**
	c. In the Look In section, **select the Eligibility.docx file and click OK.**
	d. Notice that the hyperlink is highlighted in blue to distinguish it from the rest of the text. **Save the document as _My Time Off Memo.docx_ and close it.**

TOPIC E
Add Cross-References

You have created links to specific content to add clarity to your document without repeating information. Similarly, bringing in a reference to a particular page or text on the prior pages of your document enables the reader to refer to that content in case of doubt. In this topic, you will add cross-references within your document.

You are working on your company's financial report that will be published in the monthly journal. The editor has asked you to keep the number of pages to 12. You find that you need to refer to certain charts and tables on prior pages to add clarity to the text, but adding the charts and tables to the document again would increase the page count. By using cross-references, you can add clarity to the text while still maintaining your desired page count.

Cross-References

Definition:

A *cross-reference* is a phrase that directs the reader to a particular location in a document. It always indicates content that is related to, but is not adjacent to, the content that the reader is looking at. A cross-reference can refer to text, graphics, tables, or pictures. Cross-references can be added as hyperlinks.

Example:

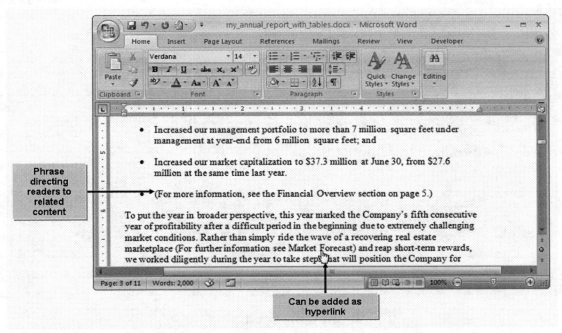

The Cross-Reference Dialog Box

The Cross-Reference dialog box contains options to insert a cross-reference to text or other objects in a document.

The following table describes the options available in the Cross-reference dialog box.

Option	Description
Reference Type	Displays a list of items you may want to reference.
Insert Reference To	Displays a list of information you may want to insert in the cross-reference. The options displayed depend upon the reference type selected.
Insert As Hyperlink	Enables users to add the cross-reference as a hyperlink that directs the user to the location specified in the cross-reference.
For Which [Object]	Displays the list of items available in the document for the selected reference type.

How to Add Cross-References

Procedure Reference: Insert and Update Cross-References

To insert and update cross-references:

1. Place the insertion point at the location where you want to insert the cross-reference.
2. Type the text that will precede the cross-reference.
3. On the Insert tab, in the Links group, click Cross-Reference to display the Cross-Reference dialog box.
4. From the Reference Type drop-down list, select the type of item you want to reference.
5. From the Insert Reference To drop-down list, select the type of item you want to insert in the document.
6. If necessary, check the Insert As Hyperlink check box.
7. In the For Which [Object] list box, select the specific item the cross-reference needs to refer to.

 Some reference types, such as figures, require a caption for them to be displayed in the For Which list box.

8. Click Insert to place the cross-reference.

 You can make cross-references and other fields appear shaded all the time. To do so, in the Advanced category in the Word Options dialog box, in the Show Document Content section, from the Field Shading drop-down list, select Always.

9. Click Close to close the Cross-Reference dialog box.
10. If necessary, finish typing the remaining text supporting the cross-reference.
11. If necessary, Ctrl-click the cross-reference to navigate to the cross-referenced location.

12. If necessary, update the cross-reference.
    - Right-click the cross-reference and choose Update Field to update the current cross-reference.
    - Or, select the entire document and press F9 to update all the fields in the document.

ACTIVITY 4-5
Inserting Cross-References

Data Files:

Annual Report with Tables.docx

Before You Begin:

From the C:\084895Data\Adding Reference Marks and Notes folder, open Annual Report with Tables.docx.

Display the Document Map pane.

Scenario:

You need to direct the readers' attention to headings, figures, and tables in the stockholder report. You can type textual references in the report, such as "See Figure 1", but you realize that if the document changes, the textual reference may no longer be accurate.

What You Do	How You Do It
1. **Cross-reference the "Financial Overview" heading in the last bullet point below the "Fiscal Accomplishments" title.**	a. **Display the Bookmark dialog box.**
	b. **Navigate to the Fiscal bookmark and close the dialog box.**
	c. **Place the insertion point at the end of the last bullet point and press Enter.**
	d. **Type *(For more information, see the* and press the Spacebar.**
	e. On the Insert tab, in the Links group, **click Cross-Reference.**
	f. In the Cross-Reference dialog box, from the Reference Type drop-down list, **select Heading.**
	g. In the For Which Heading list box, **select Financial Overview and click Insert.**
	h. **Click Close** to close the Cross-Reference dialog box.
	i. **Press the Spacebar and type *section.)*** to complete the supporting text after the Financial Overview cross-reference.
	j. **Ctrl-click the Financial Overview link** to display the Financial Overview section on page 5.

2. **Cross-reference Figure 1.**

    a. In the Document Map pane, **click "Strategy".**

    b. In the third line of the paragraph, **place the insertion point before the sentence that begins with "More than providing".**

    c. **Type *(See* and press the Spacebar.**

    d. **Display the Cross-Reference dialog box.**

    e. From the Reference Type drop-down list, **select Figure.**

    f. From the Insert Reference To drop-down list, **select Only Label And Number.**

    g. In the For Which Caption list box, **verify that "Figure 1: Teamwork is critical to our success." is selected.**

    h. **Click Insert and close the Cross-Reference dialog box.**

    i. After the Figure 1 cross-reference, **type *.)* and press the Spacebar** to complete the supporting text.

3. **Cross-reference Table 1.**

    a. In the Document Map pane, **click Residential.**

    b. In the third line of the paragraph, **place the insertion point before the sentence that begins with "This ongoing trend".**

    c. **Type *(See the data in* and press the Spacebar.**

    d. **Display the Cross-Reference dialog box.**

    e. From the Reference Type drop-down list, **select Table.**

    f. From the Insert Reference To drop-down list, **select Only Label And Number.**

    g. In the For Which Caption list box, **verify that "Table 1: The North regularly lags behind." is selected.**

    h. **Click Insert and close the Cross-Reference dialog box.**

    i. After the Table 1 cross-reference, **type *.)* and press the Spacebar** to complete the supporting text.

    j. **Save the document as *My Annual Report with Tables.docx* and close it.**

TOPIC F

Add Citations and a Bibliography

You know how to provide cross-references for content that is in another part of a document. In the course of your work, you may have referred to various documentation when creating your document. The credibility of your document is also dependent on the references that you provide during document creation. In this topic, you will add citations and a bibliography.

Just as the validity of a news story is dependent on the sources the journalist interviewed, the relevance of content in a document is dependent on the references researched. Therefore, it becomes necessary for you to give readers credible references. Word 2007 simplifies this process by enabling you to enter citations throughout a document, which will allow for the creation of a bibliography using a single command.

Sources

A *source* is reference material from which content is borrowed. Content from a source can include specific material such as text, graphics, pictures, or tables from the source, or it can include the entire source itself.

Citations

A *citation* is a reference to any legal source of content. You can use the Insert Citation command to create a citation. Citations can be made in the body of the text or in footnotes found at the bottom of a page.

Bibliographies

A *bibliography* is the list of references that is usually inserted at the end of a section or document. Bibliographic content helps identify the editions, dates of issue, authorship, and typography of books or other written material.

Bibliography Citation Styles

Bibliography citation styles provide a consistent appearance to the reference information in a document. Word 2007 provides users with numerous built-in reference styles.

Style	Description
APA	The APA or American Psychological Association style is usually used as a reference style in psychological, educational, and other social-sciences-based documents.
Chicago	The Chicago Manual of Style is usually used in noneducational documents such as magazines and newspapers.
GB7714	GB7714 is a style type followed by the Standardization Administration of China.
GOST – Name Sort	GOST – Name Sort is a style type followed by The Federal Agency of the Russian Federation on Technical Regulating and Metrology.

Style	Description
GOST – Title Sort	GOST – Title Sort is a style type followed by The Federal Agency of the Russian Federation on Technical Regulating and Metrology.
ISO 690 – First Element And Date	ISO 690 – First Element And Date is a style type followed by the International Organization for Standardization.
ISO 690 – Numerical Reference	ISO 690 – Numerical Reference is a style type followed by the International Organization for Standardization.
MLA	The MLA or Modern Language Association Style is used in documents related to literature, arts, and humanities.
SIST02	SIST02 is also called the Standards for Information of Science and Technology Style. This style is used mostly in Asian countries.
Turabian	Turabian Style is used by students for their academic documents.

How to Add Citations and a Bibliography

Procedure Reference: Insert a Citation

To insert a citation:

1. Place the insertion point at the location where you want to insert the citation.
2. On the References tab, in the Citations & Bibliography group, from the Style drop-down list, select a style.
3. Click Insert Citation and choose an appropriate option.
   - Choose Add New Source, and in the Create Source dialog box, specify the options in order to add the information.
      a. From the Type Of Source drop-down list, select the appropriate source.
      b. Based on the type of source, fill in the bibliography fields.
      c. If necessary, check the Show All Bibliography Fields check box.
      d. Click OK to close the dialog box.
   - Or, choose Add New Placeholder, and in the Placeholder Name dialog box, type a name for the placeholder and click OK to add a placeholder to fill in the information later.

The Create Source Dialog Box

The Create Source dialog box contains options that enable you to create a new source for a citation and a bibliography. The options available for creating a source vary depending on the reference style selected.

The options in the Create Source dialog box are described in the following table.

Option	Description
Type Of Source	Displays a list of source types from which the content has been borrowed.
Bibliography Fields	Enables users to enter information about the source.

Option	Description
Show All Bibliography Fields	Displays all the fields related to the reference style and source selected.
Tag Name	Identifies a particular source.

Procedure Reference: Add a Bibliography

To add a bibliography:

1. Click at the end of the document.
2. On the References tab, in the Citations & Bibliography group, click Bibliography and choose Insert Bibliography, or, in the Built-In section, choose Bibliography.

 To insert a bibliography, the user must already have inserted a source using the Create Source dialog box.

Procedure Reference: Modify a Source

To modify a source:

1. Place the mouse pointer over the citation source or placeholder to display the field.
2. Right-click the citation, source, or placeholder and choose Edit Source.
3. In the Edit Source dialog box, add or modify the details.
4. Click OK.

The Edit Source Dialog Box

Whenever you wish to modify the information about a source, you can display the Edit Source dialog box. The options in the Edit Source dialog box are similar to the options in the Create Source dialog box.

Procedure Reference: Modify a Citation

To modify a citation:

1. Place the mouse pointer over the citation source or placeholder to display the field.
2. Right-click the citation and choose Edit Citation.
3. In the Edit Citation dialog box, set options.
   - In the Add section, in the Pages text box, type the pages that you wish to include as part of the citation.
   - In the Suppress section, check the check box to prevent author, year, or title information from being displayed.
4. Click OK.

The Edit Citation Dialog Box

You can use the Edit Citation dialog box to include the pages you want to refer to along with the citation. In addition, you can prevent author, year, and title information from being displayed in the document.

Procedure Reference: Modify a Bibliography

To modify a bibliography:

1. On the References tab, in the Citations & Bibliography group, click Manage Sources.
2. In the Source Manager dialog box, in the Sources Available In section, in the Current list box, select the source and click Edit.
3. In the Edit Source dialog box, modify the details.
4. Click OK to close the Edit Source dialog box.
5. Click Close to close the Source Manager dialog box.
6. Press F9 to update the bibliography field.

The Source Manager Dialog Box

The Source Manager dialog box is used to filter the source that is to be added as a bibliographic reference from the various sources added to the document. Using the options in the Search section, you can search for a specific source type based on author, tag, title, or year information. The Sources Available In section displays the list of sources available in the master and current documents. Using the options here, you can also copy source content from the Master List to the Current List, delete any particular source, edit source information, or create a new source. The Preview section displays the style in which the source will be displayed, both as a citation and a bibliography.

ACTIVITY 4-6

Adding Citations and a Bibliography

Data Files:

Financial Report.docx

Before You Begin:

From the C:\084895Data\Adding Reference Marks and Notes folder, open Financial Report.docx.

Scenario:

You have compiled the financial report for your company's online journal by procuring information from the finance and administrative departments. You want to acknowledge these sources of information in your document to ensure that there are no legal issues with your document. In instances where you are not sure of the department you obtained the information, you decide to include placeholders.

What You Do	How You Do It
1. Designate Samantha Smith as a source.	a. **Navigate to the title "Economic Indicators On The Web".**
	b. In the first line, **click after the text "The Economic Indicators Web site".**
	c. On the References tab, in the Citations & Bibliography group, from the Style drop-down list, **select Chicago.**
	d. **Click Insert Citation and choose Add New Source.**
	e. In the Create Source dialog box, from the Type Of Source drop-down list, **select Report.**
	f. In the Author text box, **type *Samantha Smith***
	g. In the Title text box, **type *Economics Review 2005***
	h. In the Year text box, **type *June, 2005* and click OK.**
	i. Notice that (Smith June, 2005) appears beside the text "The Economic Indicators Web site", indicating the addition of the citation.
2. Insert a placeholder to mark the "Net Income" citation.	a. **Navigate to the title Net Income.**
	b. **Place the insertion point at the end of the first paragraph.**
	c. In the Citations & Bibliography group, **click Insert Citation and choose Add New Placeholder.**
	d. In the Placeholder Name dialog box, **verify that the name of the placeholder is indicated as Placeholder1 and click OK.**

3. **Designate Mike Nash as a source.**

   a. **Navigate to the end of the document.**

   b. **Display the Create Source dialog box.**

   c. From the Type Of Source drop-down list, **select Web Site.**

   d. In the Author text box, **type *Mike Nash***

   e. In the Name Of Web Page text box, **type *Economic Indicators***

   f. In the URL text box, **type *www.economicindicators.example* and click OK.**

4. **Insert a bibliography.**

   a. **Verify that the insertion point is at the end of the document and press Enter.**

   b. In the Citations & Bibliography group, **click Bibliography and choose Bibliography** to add the bibliography at the end of the document.

ACTIVITY 4-7

Modifying Citations and a Bibliography

Before You Begin:

Financial Report.docx is open.

Scenario:

You just received the financial report from your editor. She has pointed out a few issues that need to be updated in the document before sending the document back to her. She has asked you to cite the year in which the content was updated on the website. Apart from this, she has suggested that including the author name for the economic review is not necessary. Also, you need to update the placeholder so that she can include the report in the journal.

What You Do	How You Do It
1. Update the placeholder.	a. Navigate to the title Net Income, right-click Placeholder1, and choose Edit Source.
	b. In the Edit Source dialog box, from the Type Of Source drop-down list, **select Book.**
	c. In the Author text box, **type *Ashton, Chris***
	d. In the Year text box, **type *Jan, 2006* and click OK.**
	e. Notice that the text Placeholder1 is now updated with (Chris Jan, 2006).
2. Hide the author information.	a. **Navigate to the "Economic Indicators On The Web" paragraph.**
	b. In the first line of the paragraph, **right-click the citation and choose Edit Citation.**
	c. In the Edit Citation dialog box, in the Suppress section, **check the Author check box.**
	d. **Click OK** to close the Edit Citation dialog box.

3. **Update the bibliography informa-tion for Mike Nash.**

    a. On the References tab, in the Citations & Bibliography group, **click Manage Sources.**

    b. In the Source Manager dialog box, in the Sources Available In section, in the Current List list box, **select Nash, Mike and click Edit.**

    c. In the Edit Source dialog box, in the Year text box, **type *Feb, 2006* and click OK.**

    d. In the Microsoft Office Word warning message box, **click Yes.**

    e. **Click Close** to close the Source Manager dialog box.

4. **Update the references.**

    a. **Select the entire document.**

    b. **Press F9** to update the references.

    c. **Scroll down** to the end of the document to view the updated bibliography.

    d. **Save the document as *My Financial Report.docx* and close it.**

Lesson 4 Follow-up

In this lesson, you added descriptive reference marks. Footnotes, endnotes, citations, and bibliographies supply the reader with detailed explanations and source information, while bookmarks and hyperlinks enable users to navigate quickly and easily to marked locations. Captions and cross-references aid in increased understanding of the content.

1. **Considering the types of documents you currently produce, how might you use reference marks and notes to make document information more accessible for readers?**

2. **Of the different types of reference marks and notes, which ones are you most likely to use in your documents?**

5 | Making Long Documents Easier to Use

Lesson Time: 1 hour(s), 10 minutes

Lesson Objectives:

In this lesson, you will make long documents easier to use.

You will:

- Insert blank pages and cover pages.
- Insert an index.
- insert a table of figures.
- Insert a table of authorities.
- Insert a table of contents.
- Create a master document.
- Automatically summarize a document.

Introduction

You have explained content and added source information about specific content using reference marks and notes. Now, you want to help readers locate specific figures, tables, graphics, or text in a document. In this lesson, you will use various techniques that help make long documents easier to use.

You have compiled a 100 page report on your latest project. Your colleague has asked you for certain information regarding your project. Though you have documented that information, you are not sure of the page or the section it is available in. By inserting a reference table that lists the contents with their corresponding location, you will be able to locate required information quickly.

TOPIC A
Insert Blank and Cover Pages

Scrolling through pages and pages of document content can quickly become a chore. By breaking the monotony, you can retain the user's interest in your document. In this topic, you will insert blank and cover pages.

When you walk into a store, the first thing that attracts you to a product is its packaging. Likewise, the value of your documents is usually judged by their cover pages. Word offers a range of built-in cover page options that can help you create and format your cover pages with ease.

How to Insert Blank Pages and Cover Pages

Procedure Reference: Insert Blank or Cover Pages

To insert blank or cover pages:

1. Place the insertion point at the appropriate location.
   - Place the insertion point at the beginning of the document to insert a cover page.
   - Place the insertion point before or after the text or page where you want to insert the blank page.
2. Insert a page using the Pages group on the Insert tab.
   - From the Cover Page gallery, select the desired style and type the desired content to create a cover page.
   - Click Blank Page to insert a blank page.

 When you try to insert a blank page before a section break, Word inserts a page break before the section break.

ACTIVITY 5-1

Inserting Blank and Cover Pages

Data Files:

Annual Report With Tables.docx

Before You Begin:

1. From the C:\084895Data\Making Long Document Easier to Use folder, open Annual Report With Tables.docx and display the formatting marks.
2. Display the Document Map pane.

Scenario:

The financial report for the year has been updated with the latest information and is ready for print. However, when you look at the document's print preview, the document seems to start abruptly without any kind of introduction. You decide to add a cover page to the report.

What You Do	How You Do It
1. Insert a cover page.	a. **Verify that the mouse pointer is placed at the beginning of the document.**
	b. On the Insert tab, in the Pages group, from the Cover Page gallery, **select Cubicles.**
	c. **Click the text "Type The Company Name" and type** *Burke Properties*
	d. **Scroll down, click the text "Type The Document Title" and type** *Burke Properties, Inc.*
	e. **Click the text "Type The Document Subtitle" and type** *Annual Report*
	f. **Click the text "Type The Author Name" and type** *Justine Altman*
	g. **Click the text "Year" and, from the date field placeholder drop-down list, select the current date.**

2. Insert a blank page.

    a. **Scroll down and place the insertion point before the heading "Burke Properties, Inc."**

    b. In the Pages group, **click Blank Page** to insert a blank page.

    c. **Save the file as *My Annual Report with Tables.docx***

TOPIC B

Insert an Index

You have inserted a cover page and a blank page. Now, in order to complete the document, you want to provide a detailed listing of the important terms in the document, along with their page numbers, so that people can refer to the listing to locate information. In this topic, you will insert an index.

Providing an index gives readers a way to locate marked entries wherever they appear in a document. When you use Word to insert an index, the index is automatically updated whenever a document's text or pagination changes.

The Mark Index Entry Dialog Box

The Mark Index Entry dialog box contains options to locate and mark text in a document as entries in the index.

The following table describes the sections available in the Mark Index Entry dialog box.

Section	Description
Index	Enables the user to specify the main index entry text and the subentries.
Options	Enables the user to specify the type of the selected index entry. The index entry type could be a cross-reference, the current page, or a specific page range.
Page Number Format	Enables the user to specify the Font Style of the page numbers in the document.

Mark Index Entries Options

By default, index entries use the Current Page option in order to identify the marked term or phrase as being on that particular page. However, you can also use the Cross-Reference or Page Range Bookmark option. The Cross-Reference option allows you to redirect the reader to another term in the index. For example, if the reader looks up the word "Colonial" in the index, you can use the Cross-Reference option to insert "See Housing Types" to redirect the reader to the "Housing Types" index entry. The Page Range Bookmark option allows you to index a term that is used in several pages of the document.

The Concordance File

A *concordance file* is a document with a two-column table used to mark index entries automatically in another document. The first column lists the terms and phrases you want marked as index entries. These terms and phrases are entered exactly as they appear in the document to be marked. The second column contains the actual index entries for the text in the first column.

Must be created first.

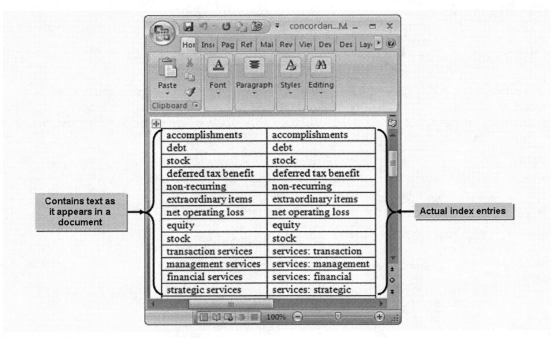

Figure 5-1: *A concordance file with index entries.*

Subentries

An index usually contains a main entry and one or more subentries. The main entries could be the headings in a document, whereas subentries are other information in the document that you may want to read about in relation to the main entry.

The Index Dialog Box

The Index dialog box enables the user to insert, format, and modify the index.

The following table describes the options available in the Index dialog box.

Option	Description
Print Preview	Displays a preview of how the content is displayed in the document.
Type	Enables the user to determine the manner in which the text in the index is to be displayed. The text can either be listed or run-in as continuous entries.
Columns	Enables the user to select and insert the desired number of columns the index will contain.
Language	Enables the user to set the desired language for the index entry.
Right Align Page Numbers	Aligns the page numbers in the index toward the right margin of the document.
Tab Leader	Enables the user to set the desired tab leader.
Formats	Enables the user to format the index.
Mark Entry	Displays the Mark Index Entry dialog box.
AutoMark	Enables Word to automatically mark new entries for the index.

Option	Description
Modify	Displays the Style dialog box with options for formatting the text entries in the index.

 In the Index dialog box, when you select Indented, the marked content is listed based on hierarchy. If you select Run-in, the content will be displayed as continuous text with one entry following the other on the same line.

The Open Index AutoMark File Dialog Box

The Open Index AutoMark File dialog box enables the user to navigate to and open the concordance file. Opening the concordance file automatically marks the text in the concordance file as entries for the index in the current document.

The Style Dialog Box

The Style dialog box contains various options to format the style of an index.

The following table describes the options available in the Style dialog box.

Option	Description
Styles	Displays a list of default index styles available in the document.
Preview	Displays a preview of the selected style.
Modify	Displays the Modify Style dialog box with options for modifying the selected index style.

The Modify Style Dialog Box

The Modify Style dialog box contains additional options to format an index.

The following table describes the options available in the Modify Style dialog box.

Option	Description
Properties	Displays the name of the selected index style, type of style, origin format, and the style followed in the paragraph following the index entry.
Formatting	Enables the user to format the index entry by specifying the font, font size, font styles, and font color.
Alignment	Enables the user to format the text alignment, spacing, and indentation of the index entry.
Preview	Displays a preview of the formatting set for the index entry.

Option	Description
Add To Quick Style List	Enables the user to add the currently set format as a style in the Quick Style list.
Automatically Update	Enables the user to automatically update the formatting style of the entries in other indices as well.
Only In This Document	Enables the user to specify that the formatting options set are for the current document only.
New Documents Based On This Template	Enables the user to set the current format of the index entries as a template for use in other documents.

How to Insert an Index

Procedure Reference: Mark Text for Indexing

To mark text for indexing:

1. Mark text.
   - Mark text manually.
     a. Select the text that you wish to mark as an index entry.
     b. On the References tab, in the Index group, click Mark Entry or press Alt+Shift+X to display the Mark Index Entry dialog box.
     c. If necessary, in the Main Entry text box, modify the content of the entry.
     d. If necessary, in the Subentry text box, type the subentry to the main index entry.
     e. In the Options section, set the type of index entry for the selected text.
     f. If necessary, in the Page Number Format section, apply a font style to the entry.
     g. Click Mark to mark that specific entry or click Mark All to mark similar entries in the document.
     h. If necessary, mark other text entries.
     i. Click Close to close the Mark Index Entry dialog box.
   - Mark text automatically.
     a. On the References tab, in the Index group, click Insert Index.
     b. In the Index dialog box, click AutoMark.
     c. In the Open Index AutoMark File dialog box, navigate to and select the concordance file and click Open.
2. If necessary, modify the document.
   a. If necessary, display the formatting marks and the Document Map pane.
   b. Navigate to the index entry you wish to modify.
   c. In the entry's field code, edit any text within the quotation marks.
3. If necessary, delete an index entry.
   a. If necessary, display the formatting marks.
   b. Scroll down to the desired index entry field code, select it, and press Delete.

Index Entry Field Codes

When you mark an index entry, the entry is represented by a field code that is displayed when the formatting mark option is enabled. The field code displays the index entry within quotes and the term XE precedes the index entry. To edit the index entry without making changes to the text content, you need to change the text within the quotes in the field code.

Procedure Reference: Insert an Index

To insert an index:

1. Place the insertion point where you want to insert the index.
2. On the References tab, in the Index group, click Insert Index.
3. In the Index dialog box, set the desired options.
4. If necessary, mark an entry for the index.
   - Click Mark Entry to display the Mark Index Entry dialog box and manually mark more entries for the index.
   - Or, click AutoMark to automatically mark index entries.
5. If necessary, click Modify to modify the formatting of the index.
   a. In the Style dialog box, select the desired index style and click Modify.
   b. In the Modify Style dialog box, set the desired formatting options.
   c. Click OK to close the Modify Style dialog box.
   d. Click OK to close the Style dialog box.
6. Click OK to insert the index.
7. If necessary, update the index.
   a. Locate the index you wish to update.
   b. Update the index.
      - Right-click the index and choose Update Field.
      - Select the index entries and press F9.
      - Or, on the References tab, in the Index group, click Update Index.

ACTIVITY 5-2

Indexing a Document

Data Files:

Concordance File.docx

Before You Begin:

My Annual Report With Tables.docx is open.

Scenario:

The annual report is complete. Now you have to add the various reference tables, such as the index.

What You Do	How You Do It
1. Mark all instances of the word "commercial", so that it appears as a subentry for services.	a. Using the Document Map pane, **navigate to the "Milestones" heading.**
	b. In the second line of the paragraph below the "Milestones" heading, **select the word "commercial".**
	c. On the References tab, in the Index group, **click Mark Entry.**
	d. In the Mark Index Entry dialog box, in the Main Entry text box, **type *Services* and press Tab.**
	e. In the Subentry text box, **type *commercial***
	f. In the Options section, **verify that Current Page is selected.**
	g. **Click Mark All and then click Close.**

2. AutoMark the rest of the document using the concordance file.

a. In the Index group, **click Insert Index.**

b. In the Index dialog box, **click AutoMark.**

c. In the Open Index AutoMark File dialog box, **navigate to the C:\084895Data\ Making Long Documents Easier To Use folder.**

d. In the Open Index AutoMark File dialog box, from the Files Of Type drop-down list, **select All Word Documents.**

e. **Notice that the terms "accomplishments," "non-recurring," "debt," and "equity" are marked.**

---

3. Insert the index.

a. Using the Document Map pane, **navigate to "Index".**

b. **Place the insertion point in the blank line after the Index title.**

c. In the Index group, **click Insert Index.**

d. In the Index dialog box, **check the Right Align Page Numbers check box.**

e. In the Formats drop-down list, **verify that From Template is selected.**

f. **Click Modify** to display the Style dialog box.

g. In the Styles list box, **verify that Index 1 is selected and click Modify.**

h. In the Modify Style dialog box, in the Formatting section, **click the first drop-down arrow, select Arial Narrow, and click OK.**

i. **Click OK** to close the Style dialog box.

j. **Click OK** to insert the index.

k. **Save the file.**

TOPIC C
Insert Table of Figures

By adding an index, you made looking up content in a document easier. Now, you need to make looking up figures in a document easier. In this topic, you will insert a table of figures.

Your annual report contains nearly one hundred figures—many of which are bar charts showing quarterly results. Instead of scrolling through the document looking at each chart, reading each caption, you just refer to the document's table of figures. Like an index, inserting a table of figures is just another way to make long documents easier to use.

The Table Of Figures Dialog Box

The Table Of Figures dialog box contains options to insert, format, and modify a table of figures.

The following table describes the option in the Table Of Figures dialog box.

Option	Description
Print Preview	Displays a preview to show how the table of figures appears in a printed Word document.
Web Preview	Displays a preview of how the table of figures appears in a web page.
Show Page Numbers	Enables the user to display the page numbers in the table of figures.
Right Align Page Numbers	Enables the user to align the page numbers to the right of the caption titles.
Tab Leader	Enables the user to set tab leader formats for the page numbers.
Use Hyperlinks Instead Of Page Numbers	Displays the listed page references in the table of figures as a hyperlink so that the user can click the desired link to navigate to that particular page.
Formats	Enables the user to format the table of figures.
Caption Label	Enables the user to insert a different caption label that is to be displayed in the table of figures. The user can also choose none so that no label is included in the table.
Include Label And Number	Displays the label and caption number in the table of figures.
Options	Displays the Table Of Figures Options dialog box. This dialog box consists of three options that enable the user to specify the content which is to be included as an entry in the table of figures. The user can also specify a table identifier. • The Style drop-down list provides options that enable the user to choose the type of content that is to be displayed in the table of figures. • The Table Entry Field check box enables the user to specify whether Word needs to use separate fields for identifying the different tables of figures. • The Table Identifier drop-down list enables the user to set a table identifier code, which Word uses to identify the table of figures.

Option	Description
Modify	Displays the Style dialog box that enables the user to modify the style of the table of figures.

 The Caption Label drop-down list in the Table Of Figures dialog box enables you to create other types of reference tables. Choosing the Tables option from the Caption Label drop-down list enables you to create a table of tables. Likewise, to create a table of equations, you can choose the Equations option from the Caption Label drop-down list.

How to Insert a Table of Figures

Procedure Reference: Insert a Table of Figures

To insert a table of figures:

1. Place the insertion point where you want the table of figures to be located.
2. On the References tab, in the Captions group, click Insert Table Of Figures.
3. In the Table Of Figures dialog box, specify the desired options.
4. If necessary, click Options and specify the desired settings in the Table Of Figures Options dialog box.
5. If necessary, click Modify and specify the desired settings.
   a. In the Style dialog box, select the Table Of Figures style you want to change and click Modify.
   b. In the Modify Style dialog box, modify the style, as desired.
   c. Click OK.
   d. If necessary, modify other table of figures styles.
   e. Click OK.
6. Click OK to insert the table of figures.
7. If necessary, in the Microsoft Office Word message box, click OK to update an existing table of figures.

Procedure Reference: Update a Table of Figures

To update a table of figures:

1. In the document window, display the table of figures you want to update.
2. Display the Update Table Of Figures dialog box.
   - On the References tab, in the Captions group, click Update Table.
   - Right-click the table of figures and choose Update Field.
   - Or, place the insertion point in the table and press F9.
3. Select the desired update option.
   - Select the Update Page Numbers Only option to update only the page numbers in the table of figures.
   - Select the Update Entire Table option to update the entire table along with the page numbers.

4. Click OK.

ACTIVITY 5-3

Inserting a Table of Figures

Before You Begin:

My Annual Report With Tables.docx is open.

Scenario:

As you look through your report, you feel that locating document information would be easier if you added a reference table for the figures.

What You Do	How You Do It
1. Insert a table of figures below the "Figures" heading.	a. Display the Bookmark dialog box.
	b. Select Figures, click Go To, and close the Bookmark dialog box.
	c. Place the insertion point in the blank line below the Figures heading.
	d. On the References tab, in the Captions group, **click Insert Table Of Figures.**
	e. In the Table Of Figures dialog box, in the Formats drop-down list, **verify that From Template is selected.**
	f. From the Caption Label drop-down list, **select Figure.**
	g. **Click Options** to display the Table Of Figure Options dialog box.
	h. From the Table Identifier drop-down list, **select A and click OK.**
	i. **Click OK** to insert the table of figures.

2. Modify the table of figures.

a. **Display the Table Of Figures dialog box and click Modify.**

b. In the Style dialog box, in the Preview section, **click Modify.**

c. In the Modify Style dialog box, from the Font drop-down list, **select Arial Narrow and click OK.**

d. **Click OK** to close the Style dialog box.

e. In the Table Of Figures dialog box, from the Caption Label drop-down list, **select Figure and click OK.**

f. In the Microsoft Office Word message box, **click OK.**

ACTIVITY 5-4
Updating a Table of Figures

Before You Begin:
My Annual Report With Tables.docx is open.

Scenario:
Your manager has approved the annual report for finance that you have created. However, she has asked you to change the caption for Figure C and update the table of figures accordingly.

What You Do	How You Do It
1. Update the caption.	a. In the table of figures, **Ctrl-click the text "Figure C: The Relocation management team".**
	b. In the Figure C caption, **place the insertion point after the text "Relocation", press the Spacebar, and type *Services***
2. Update the table of figures.	a. **Display the Bookmark dialog box.**
	b. In the Bookmark Name list box, **verify that Figures is selected, click Go To, and close the Bookmark dialog box.**
	c. **Right-click the table of figures and choose Update Field.**
	d. In the Update Table Of Figures dialog box, **select the Update Entire Table option and click OK.**
	e. Notice that the text inserted in the caption is updated in the table of figures.
	f. **Save the file.**

TOPIC D

Insert Table of Authorities

You have inserted a table of figures to help readers locate illustrations in your document. Locating legal citations in a long document is as challenging as locating specific figures. Consequently, it is in your readers' best interests for you to identify each citation and list them in a table. In this topic, you will insert a table of authorities.

You are in a courtroom and you want to refer to a legal precedent in a document. A table of authorities provides a way to locate legal references quickly. Also, if you use Word to insert a table of authorities, Word will automatically update the table whenever a document's text or pagination changes, thereby ensuring that the table of authorities is up to date.

The Mark Citation Dialog Box

The Mark Citation dialog box enables users to mark the citations that are required before inserting a table of authorities.

The following table describes the options available in the Mark Citation dialog box.

Option	Description
Selected Text	Displays the citation text as a selection.
Category	Displays a list of authorities from which the user can select the type of authority for the selected citation.
Short Citation	Enables the user to insert a new citation in the document and search for similar text in the rest of the document.
Long Citation	Displays the details of the source for the selected citation.
Next Citation	Enables the user to navigate to the next citation in the document.
Mark	Enables the user to mark the selected citation as an entry for the table of authorities.
Mark All	Enables the user to mark all citations similar to the one entered as a main entry.
Category	Displays the Edit Category dialog box. This dialog box provides options that help replace a selected category of authority with another.

The Table Of Authorities Dialog Box

The Table Of Authorities dialog box contains options to enable the user to insert, format, and modify a table of authorities.

The following table describes the options available in the Table Of Authorities dialog box.

Option	Description
Print Preview	Displays a preview to show how the table of authorities appears in a printed document.

Option	Description
Category	Contains a list of authority types you can choose from. When chosen, all citations belonging to that category will be entered in the table of authorities.
Use Passim	Displays the word Passim next to the citation entry if the same citation has been inserted more than five times.
Keep Original Formatting	Replicates the format of the marked citations in the table of authorities, thus preventing formatting discrepancies from being created.
Tab Leader	Enables users to set tab leader formats for the page numbers in the table of authorities.
Formats	Enables users to format the table of authorities.
Mark Citation	Displays the Mark Citation dialog box that can be used to mark additional citations to be inserted in the table of authorities.
Modify	Displays the Style dialog box that enables users to modify the style of the table of authorities.

How to Insert a Table of Authorities

Procedure Reference: Mark Text for a Table of Authorities

To mark text for a table of authorities:

1. Navigate to and select the desired citation.
2. Display the Mark Citation dialog box.
   - On the References tab, in the Table Of Authorities group, click Mark Citation.
   - Or, press Alt+Shift+I.
3. If necessary, in the Selected Text text box, modify the citation.
4. If necessary, from the Category drop-down list, select the category that applies to the selected caption.
5. In the Short Citation text box, edit the citation so that it matches how you use the citation elsewhere in the document. Entering a citation in the Short Citation text box helps Word use this citation as a way to locate and mark other related citations.
6. Mark the citation.
   - Click Mark to mark the selected citation.
   - Or, click Mark All to mark all instances of that citation in the document.

 Word doesn't mark multiple citations in the same paragraph.

7. Click Close.
8. If necessary, modify the marked citation.
   a. If necessary, display the formatting marks in the document.
   b. Navigate to the citation you want to modify.
   c. In the citation's TA field code, edit the long citation text within the quotation marks.

9.   If necessary, delete the marked citation.

   a.   If necessary, display the formatting marks.

   b.   Select the field codes for the desired marked citation.

   c.   Press Delete.

Field Codes for a Marked Citation

When you mark a citation as a table of authorities entry, Word inserts a field code that resembles { TA \l "Connor v. Burke, 314 US 252 (2002)" \s "Connor v. Burke" \c 1}. The "\l" indicates the long citation, the "\s" indicates the short citation, and "\c" indicates the Cases category.

Procedure Reference: Insert a Table of Authorities

To insert a table of authorities:

1.   Place the insertion point where you want to insert the table.

2.   On the References tab, in the Table Of Authorities group, click the Insert Table Of Authorities button.

3.   In the Table Of Authorities dialog box, set the desired settings.

4.   If necessary, click Mark Citations and mark more citations.

5.   If necessary, modify the appearance of the table.

6.   Click OK to insert the table of authorities.

7.   If necessary, in the Microsoft Office Word message box, click OK to update the existing table.

 The table of authorities does not provide a hyperlink option. Therefore, the user cannot use Ctrl+click to navigate to the citation.

The Use Passim Option

In the Table Of Authorities dialog box, the Use Passim check box is checked by default. Passim means "occurs frequently." If there are five or more page references to the same marked legal citation, Word will insert the word "passim" in the table rather than the page numbers when the table of authorities is inserted.

Procedure Reference: Update a Table of Authorities

To update a table of authorities:

1.   Navigate to the table of authorities.

2.   Update the table of authorities.

   ●   Right-click the table and choose Update Field.

   ●   Place the insertion point in the table of authorities and press F9.

   ●   Or, on the References tab, in the Table Of Authorities group, click the Update Table Of Authorities button.

ACTIVITY 5-5

Inserting a Table of Authorities

Before You Begin:
My Annual Report With Tables.docx is open.

Scenario:
You are to send a report you compiled to the legal team in your firm. The report contains a couple of citations to legal cases involving the company. You need to provide an easy way to refer to those citations.

What You Do	How You Do It
1. **Mark all instances of the Smith v. Burke case.**	a. Using the Document Map pane, **navigate to the Legal Issues heading.**
	b. **Select "Smith v. Burke, F2d 201 (2003)."**
	c. On the References tab, in the Table Of Authorities group, **click Mark Citation.**
	d. In the Mark Citation dialog box, from the Category drop-down list, **verify that Cases is selected.**
	e. In the Short Citation text box, **type *Smith v. Burke***
	f. **Click Mark All.**
	g. **Close the Mark Citation dialog box and scroll to the top** to view the complete citation.

2. **Insert a table of authorities below the "Authorities" heading.**

   a. **Display the Bookmark dialog box.**

   b. **Select Authorities, click Go To, and click Close.**

   c. **Place the insertion point in the blank line below the "Authorities" heading.**

   d. On the References tab, in the Table Of Authorities group, **click the Insert Table Of Authorities button.**

   e. In the Table Of Authorities dialog box, in the Category list box, **select Cases.**

   f. In the Formats drop-down list box, **verify that From Template is selected and click OK** to insert the table of authorities.

ACTIVITY 5-6

Modifying a Table of Authorities

Before You Begin:
My Annual Report With Tables.docx is open.

Scenario:
You received the report you had compiled for your legal team from your reviewer. He has pointed out that the Smith versus Burke case had taken place in 2002 and not in 2003. Also, the formatting is inconsistent in the table. He has suggested the table's text be formatted similar to the text in the other reference tables in the document.

What You Do	How You Do It
1. **Edit the information for the Smith v. Burke case.**	a. Using the Document Map pane, **navigate to the "Legal Issues" heading.**
	b. In the first paragraph below the "Legal Issues" heading, in the second line, **select both occurrences of the text (2003) and type** *(2002)*
2. **Update the table of authorities** to reflect the change in year.	a. **Display the Bookmark dialog box, navigate to the Authorities bookmark, and close the Bookmark dialog box.**
	b. **Right-click the table of authorities and choose Update Field.**
	c. Notice that the content has been updated.
	d. **Save the file.**

3. **Format the table of authorities.**

a. **Display the Table Of Authorities dialog box.**

b. **Click Modify** to display the Style dialog box.

c. In the Styles list box, **select Table Of Authorities and then click Modify.**

d. In the Modify Style dialog box, in the Formatting section, from the first drop-down list, **select Arial Narrow and click OK.**

e. **Click OK** to close the Style dialog box.

f. **Click OK** to update the table of authorities.

g. In the Microsoft Office Word message box, **click OK.**

TOPIC E
Insert Table of Contents

You have inserted a table of authorities to help readers locate legal information in a document. You now want to include a comprehensive list of all the content included in a document. In this topic, you will insert a table of contents into a document.

Most people don't read reference books cover to cover, so you know the importance of including a table of contents. Inserting a table of contents in your long documents helps your readers to quickly find the topics they want. And, much like the other reference tables in Word, using Word to insert a table of contents ensures that it will be up to date whenever a document's text or pagination changes.

The Table Of Contents Dialog Box

The Table Of Contents dialog box contains options to insert, format, and modify a table of contents.

The following table describes the options available in the Table Of Contents dialog box.

Option	Description
Print Preview	Displays a preview to show how the table of contents appears in a printed Word document.
Web Preview	Displays a preview of how the table of contents appears in a web page.
Show Page Numbers	Enables users to display the page numbers in the table of contents.
Right Align Page Numbers	Enables users to align the page numbers to the right of the caption titles.
Tab Leader	Enables users to set tab leader formats for the page numbers.
Use Hyperlinks Instead Of Page Numbers	Displays the listed page references in the table of contents as hyperlinks so that users can click a desired link to navigate to a particular page.
Formats	Enables users to format the table of figures.
Show Levels	Enables users to determine the level of listing in the table of contents.
Options	Displays the Table Of Contents Options dialog box. This dialog box contains three options that enable users to modify the style and listing of the table of contents.
	• The Available Styles option displays a list of options from which users can choose to include styles beside the Heading Styles and also determine the level of listing.
	• The Outline Levels option enables users to modify the selected style's outline level in the Paragraph dialog box.
	• The Table Entry Fields option updates the field codes automatically to mark hierarchy.
Modify	Displays the Style dialog box that enables users to modify the style of the table of figures.

The Add Text Option

When adding an entry to the table of contents, the options in the Add Text drop-down list enable the user to decide the level of importance of a heading and list it accordingly.

Option	Description
Do Not Show In Table Of Contents	Displays no listing among the headings in the table.
Level 1	Displays the selected text in the left margin of the document.
Level 2	Displays the selected text in the margin range next to the left margin of the document.
Level 3	Displays the selected text at the third level of the hierarchy.

The Mark Table Of Contents Entry Dialog Box

The Mark Table Of Contents Entry dialog box contains options to manually mark text as an entry for the table of contents.

The following table describes the options available in the Mark Table Of Contents Entry dialog box.

Option	Description
Entry	Displays the text that is to be marked as an entry for the table of contents.
Table Identifier	Enables Word to identify the table of contents based on hierarchy.
Level	Enables the user to mark the level of listing of the selected text.
Mark	Marks the text with the specified settings as an entry for the table of contents.

How to Insert a Table of Contents

Procedure Reference: Insert a Table of Contents

To insert a table of contents using the Table Of Contents dialog box:

1. Mark entries for the table of contents.
   a. Select the desired content.
   b. Press Alt+Shift+O to display the Mark Table Of Contents Entry dialog box.
   c. If necessary, in the Entry text box, edit the entry text.
   d. If necessary, from the Table Identifier drop-down list, select the table identifier.
   e. If necessary, in the Level spin box, mark a level of listing for the selected text.
   f. Click Mark.

2. Place the insertion point where you want the table of contents to be located.

3. On the References tab, in the Table Of Contents group, from the Table Of Contents drop-down list, select Insert Table Of Contents.

4. In the Table Of Contents dialog box, specify the desired settings.
   - Check the Show Page Number check box to display the page numbers in the table of contents entries.
   - Align the page numbers.
     a. Check the Right-Align Page Numbers check box to align the page numbers to the right.
     b. From the Tab Leader drop-down list, select the desired tab leader.
   - Check the Use Hyperlinks Instead Of Page Numbers check box to insert the reference as a hyperlink.
   - If necessary, from the Formats drop-down list, select a preset table of contents design.
   - If necessary, in the Show Level spin box, specify the level settings.

5. If necessary, change the style settings for the table.

6. If necessary, modify the appearance of the table.

7. Click OK to insert the table of contents.

Procedure Reference: Update a Table of Contents

To update a table of contents:

1. Navigate to the desired table of contents.

2. Display the Update Table Of Contents dialog box.
   - Right-click the table and choose Update Field.
   - Place the insertion point in the table of contents and press F9.
   - On the References tab, in the Table Of Contents group, click Update Table.
   - Or, press Alt+S+U.

3. Specify the desired update option.
   - Select Update Page Numbers Only to update the page numbers in the table.
   - Select Update Entire Table to update the content and page numbers in the table.

4. Click OK to update the table.

If you change the entries in the table of contents directly and then update the table using the Update Table Of Contents dialog box, the changes made will be lost. However, if you make the changes to the content in the document directly and then update the table, the table of contents would be updated.

Procedure Reference: Add Entries to the Table of Contents

To add entries to the table of contents:

1. In the document, select the text you wish to add to the table.
2. On the References tab, in the Table Of Contents group, from the Add Text drop-down list, select the desired level of listing.
3. Update the table of contents.

ACTIVITY 5-7

Inserting a Table of Contents

Before You Begin:

My Annual Report With Tables.docx is open.

Scenario:

You have written a comprehensive company guide that will be distributed to all of your company's current employees. You want to provide an accurate table of contents to make it easier for the employees to quickly access the information they need. And since the document contains text formatted with Heading 1, Heading 2, and Heading 3 styles already, it shouldn't be difficult. Also, in the table of contents, the table's text should be formatted in a way that's similar to the text in the other reference tables.

What You Do	How You Do It
1. Set options for a two-level table of contents table.	a. Using the Bookmark dialog box, **navigate to the Contents bookmark and then close the dialog box.**
	b. **Place the insertion point in the blank line after the "Contents" heading.**
	c. On the References tab, in the Table Of Contents group, **click Table Of Contents and select Insert Table Of Contents.**
	d. In the Formats drop-down list box, **verify that From Template is selected.**
	e. In the Show Levels spin box, **click the down arrow button** to set the level listing to two.

2. **Format the table of contents.**

a. In the Table Of Contents dialog box, **click Modify.**

b. In the Style dialog box, in the Styles list box, **verify that TOC 1 is selected and click Modify.**

c. In the Modify Style dialog box, in the Formatting section, from the Font drop-down list, **select Arial Narrow and click OK.**

d. **Click OK** to close the Style dialog box.

e. **Click OK** to insert the table of contents.

f. **Save the document and close it.**

TOPIC F
Create a Master Document

You have inserted various reference tables in your long documents to access information more easily. An alternative would be to work with shorter documents and combine them later. In this topic, you will create a master document that consists of several subdocuments.

Your team has completed a new project and you have to submit a detailed report on the project to the board. To finish the document on time, each team member is working on a chapter of the report. By combining the chapters as subdocuments within a single master document, you can create references, such as a table of contents, for all these chapters at one time.

Master Documents

Definition:

A *master document* is a document that acts as a container for its own content and links to other related documents called subdocuments. The contents of linked subdocuments are displayed in the master document. The master document may contain any number of subdocuments. The contents can be modified either in the individual subdocuments or in the master document with those changes being reflected dynamically in the other location.

Example:

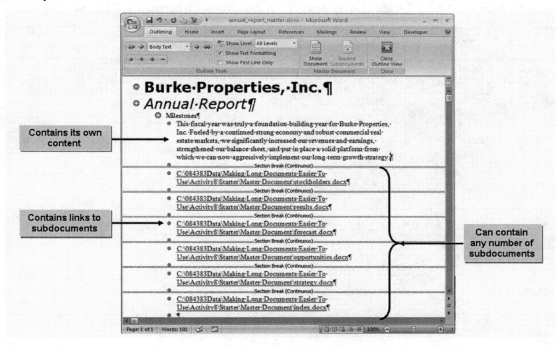

Benefits of Master Documents

Using a master document, you can separate a long document into shorter, more manageable pieces—the subdocuments. Subdocuments may be easier for you to rearrange within the master document rather than cutting and pasting or dragging sections around in Outline view. Master documents have additional benefits, such as:

● Allowing for quicker compilation of documents in a central location for easier access.

- Providing a convenient means to mark entries and insert referential tables for several documents.
- Reducing the file size because the master document doesn't actually contain the subdocument content; rather, it contains the link to the subdocuments.
- Allowing for printing of multiple documents without opening them individually.

Deleting Subdocument Links from the Main Document

You can delete the link to the subdocument from the master document. This will remove the content from the master document, but not the content in the subdocument.

The Outlining Tab

The Outlining tab appears when the document is displayed in the Outline view. This tab contains groups of options to create, edit, and format the master document.

The following table describes the groups on the Outlining tab.

Group	Description
Outline Tools	Contains options that help format the content in the master document.
Master Document	Enables the user to display or hide the content of the subdocuments. Clicking Show Document displays more options in this group.
Close	Closes Outline view and displays the document in Print Layout view.

 You can also lock the subdocuments to prevent other users from modifying the content.

How to Create a Master Document

Procedure Reference: Create a Master Document

To create a master document:

1. Open a new document and save it in the .docx format.
2. Display the document in Outline view.
   - On the View tab, in the Document Views group, click Outline.
   - Or, on the Microsoft Office Status Bar, click the Outline button.
3. If necessary, using the Outline Tools options, set the levels to be shown in the document.
4. Place the insertion point where you want to insert the subdocument.
5. In the Master Document group, click Show Documents.
6. Click Insert and navigate to and open the desired document to add it as a subdocument.
7. Add other subdocuments, as desired.
8. Save the master document.
9. If necessary, click the subdocument icon to select it and press Delete to delete the subdocument.
   a. If necessary, display the master document in Outline view.
   b. Press Delete.

Delinking Subdocuments

Once a subdocument has been inserted into the master, it becomes linked to the master and its contents can be edited directly in the master. All changes made to the subdocument in the master document are saved to the subdocument. To remove that connection and include the subdocument as part of the master document, click the desired subdocument's icon and click the Remove Subdocument button.

ACTIVITY 5-8

Creating a Master Document

Data Files:

Annual Report Master.docx, Stockholders.docx, Results.docx, Forecast.docx, Opportunities.docx, Strategy.docx, Index.docx

Before You Begin:

From the C:\084895Data\Making Long Documents Easier to Use folder, open Annual Report Master.docx.

Scenario:

You are constantly updating the annual report and the supporting documents. Rather than making changes in two places, you want to combine the supporting documents into a single document container so that when you make any changes in one place, they are reflected in the other. This will also make it easier to update any existing reference tables and indices, as needed.

What You Do	How You Do It
1. **Insert the Stockholders document as a subdocument in the Annual Report document.**	a. On the Microsoft Office Status Bar, **click the Outline button.**
	b. **Place the insertion point at the end of the document.**
	c. On the Outlining tab, in the Master Document group, **click Show Document** to display the additional options in the group.
	d. **Click Insert** and, in the Insert Subdocument dialog box, **navigate to the C:\084895Data\Making Long Documents Easier to Use folder.**
	e. **Select the Stockholders.docx document and click Open.**

2. **Insert the other supporting docu-ments as subdocuments below the Stockholders subdocument.**

    a. **Verify that the insertion point is at the end of the document.**

    b. In the Master Document group, **click Insert.**

    c. **Open the Results.docx document.**

    d. **Click Insert and open the Forecast.docx document.**

    e. Similarly, **add the Opportunities.docx, Strategy.docx, and Index.docx docu-ments** as subdocuments.

    f. **Save the master document as** *My Annual Report Master.docx*

    g. In the Master Document group, **click Col-lapse Subdocuments.**

    h. Notice that the path and file names for the subdocuments are indicated as links.

ACTIVITY 5-9

Modifying the Master Document

Before You Begin:

My Annual Report Master.docx is open.

Scenario:

You sent the master document that you had compiled for review to your manager. She sent the document back to you asking you to change the Strategy heading in the Strategy subdocument to Policy. She also requested you to delete the Forecast document.

What You Do	How You Do It
1. **Modify the heading "Strategy".**	a. On the Outlining tab, in the Master Document group, **click Expand Subdocuments and display the document in Print Layout view.**
	b. Using the Document Map pane, **navigate to the Strategy heading.**
	c. **Select the Strategy heading and type *Policy***
	d. **Open the Stockholders.docx document.**
	e. **Scroll down** to verify that the third heading has been changed to Policy.
	f. **Close the document.**
2. In the master document, **delete the Forecast subdocument.**	a. Using the Document Map pane, **navigate to the Market Forecast heading.**
	b. **Display the document in Outline view.**
	c. To the left of the "Market Forecast" heading, **click the subdocument icon and press Delete.**
	d. **Save and close the document.**
	e. **Close the Document Map.**

TOPIC G

Automatically Summarize a Document

You have compiled a master document that contains several subdocuments. You may now want to provide the reader with a summary of the document's contents. In this topic, you will autosummarize a document.

The Chief Financial Officer has been asked to give the opening speech to the shareholders. She wants to refer to the annual report's key points, but she doesn't have the time to read the entire document. She asks for you to provide her with an executive summary as soon as possible. You can simply use Word to automatically summarize the document.

The AutoSummarize Dialog Box

The AutoSummarize dialog box contains a group of options and formats that you can use to create a summary of a document.

The following table describes the sections of the AutoSummarize dialog box.

Section	Description
Type Of Summary	Enables users to select the desired summary type.
Length Of Summary	Enables users to set the length of the summary. This section also contains options that enable users to determine the percentage of original content to be used in the summary.
Update Document Statistics	Updates statistical information, such as the document word count, automatically.

Types of Summary

You can autosummarize a document in four different ways:

- Highlight Key Points: Examines the document and highlights the most relevant sentences.
- Create A New Document And Put The Summary There: Inserts the key point summary in a separate document.
- Insert An Executive Summary Or Abstract At The Top Of The Document: Inserts the key point summary at the beginning of the document below the word "Summary", which is formatted with the Heading 1 style.
- Hide Everything But The Summary Without Leaving The Original Document: Displays only the document's key point summary.

AutoSummary Tools

The AutoSummary Tools option enables the user to automatically summarize a document.

Option	Description
Auto Summarize	Displays the Auto Summarize dialog box that enables the user to automatically summarize the document.
Resummarize	Enables the user to resummarize the document if changes have been made to the content after using the AutoSummarize option.
Highlight/Show Only Summary	Enables the user to either highlight the summary content in the original document or display only the summary content.
Close	Closes the AutoSummary Tools options.

How to Automatically Summarize a Document

Procedure Reference: Automatically Summarize a Document

To automatically summarize a document:

1. If necessary, add the AutoSummary Tools command to the Quick Access toolbar.
2. On the Quick Access toolbar, click the AutoSummary Tools button and choose Auto Summarize.
3. In the AutoSummarize dialog box, in the Type Of Summary section, select the desired style.
4. In the Length Of Summary section, from the Percent Of Original drop-down list, select the percentage of the original content to be used in the summary content.
5. If necessary, uncheck the Update Document Statistics check box to keep the comments and keywords that are currently stored in the document's Properties dialog box.
6. Click OK to summarize the document.

ACTIVITY 5-10

Summarizing a Document Automatically

Data Files:

Report Text.docx

Before You Begin:

From the C:\084895Data\Making Long Documents Easier to Use folder, open Report Text.docx.

Scenario:

Your manager has read the project report and has asked you to provide her with a summary document that contains some of the report's key points. She particularly wants to use some of the bullet points from the Stockholder's section. She doesn't care how the summary document is formatted because she needs the document quickly.

What You Do	How You Do It
1. **Highlight the key points in the report.**	a. **Add the AutoSummary Tools command to the Quick Access toolbar.**
	b. On the Quick Access toolbar, **click the AutoSummary Tools button** [icon] **and choose Auto Summarize.**
	c. In the AutoSummarize dialog box, in the Type Of Summary section, **verify that the Highlight Key Points option is selected.**
	d. **Click OK** to highlight the key points.
2. **Insert the summary in a new document.**	a. **Display the AutoSummarize dialog box.**
	b. In the Type Of Summary section, **select the Create A New Document And Put The Summary There option and click OK.**
	c. **Save the new document as** *My Summary.docx* **and close it.**
	d. **Close the Report Text document without saving it.**

Lesson 5 Follow-up

In this lesson, you made locating content in long documents easier by identifying words and legal cases to be included in the index and table of authorities, respectively. Furthermore, you inserted reference tables for contents, figures, and data tables, thereby allowing readers to quickly view those objects. You met the challenge of managing sections of long documents by utilizing existing documents to create a master document. In addition, you automatically summarized the master document by highlighting its key points.

1. **What types of long documents are you likely to create on your job?**

2. **How would you make your long documents easier to use?**

6 | Securing a Document

Lesson Time: 1 hour(s)

Lesson Objectives:

In this lesson, you will secure a document.

You will:

- Update a document's properties.
- Hide text.
- Remove personal information from a document.
- Set formatting and editing restrictions for a document.
- Add a digital signature to a document.
- Use a password to open a document.
- Restrict document access.

Introduction

Now that your document is complete with a table of contents and other table references, you may want to distribute it. But, before that, you may need to prevent unauthorized access or changes to the content in the document. In this lesson, you will secure a document.

Assume you have created a report on the history of legal cases involving your company over the past decade. Since this report contains confidential information, you may need to ensure that no one but the authorized people are able to access it. By using the security features in Microsoft® Office Word, you can accomplish this.

TOPIC A

Update a Document's Properties

You have seen how your personal information can be used in a document, but, in some cases, you may need to provide additional information. In this topic, you will add more descriptive details to the document's properties.

Your manager has asked you to update the 50 page accounting procedures document that was created sometime last year. You don't want to retype the whole document. However, you want the updates you make to be attributed to you. By changing the document's properties, you can do just that.

How to Update a Document's Properties

Procedure Reference: Update a Document's Properties

To update a document's properties:

1. Click the Office button and choose Prepare→Properties.
2. Click Document Properties and choose Advanced Properties.
3. If necessary, update the summary information.
    a. Select the Summary tab.
    b. If necessary, delete the existing information in the desired text boxes.
    c. Type in the summary information in the desired text boxes.
4. If necessary, update the custom information.
    a. Select the Custom tab.
    b. In the Name list box, select a built-in property name or, in the Name text box, type the name for a new custom property.
    c. If necessary, from the Type drop-down list, select the desired content type of the custom property.
    d. In the Value text box, type the value of the custom property.

 If you select Yes Or No as the type of the custom property, the Value section displays Yes and No options, with the Yes option selected by default.

    e. Click Add.
5. Click OK.
6. Save the document to store the new properties.

ACTIVITY 6-1

Updating a Document's Properties

Data Files:

Completed Annual Report.docx

Before You Begin:

From the C:\084895Data\Securing a Document folder, open Completed Annual Report.docx.

Scenario:

After the annual report was completed, the editor, Mary Coleman, read and signed off on the document. Since Mary will now be responsible for the document internally, you will update the document's properties so that she is listed as the author as well as the editor. You also want the document's properties to reflect that the document has been approved for printing.

What You Do	How You Do It
1. Change the Author information from Justine Altman to Mary Coleman.	a. Click the Office button and choose **Prepare→Properties** to display the Document Information panel.
	b. In the Document Information panel, **triple-click in the Author text box and type** *Mary Coleman*
2. Add a custom property specifying Mary Coleman as the editor.	a. **Click Document Properties.**
	b. **Choose Advanced Properties** to display the Completed Annual Report.docx Properties dialog box.
	c. **Select the Custom tab** and in the Name list box, **scroll down and select Editor.**
	d. **Verify that, in the Type drop-down list, Text is selected.**
	e. In the Value text box, **type** *Mary Coleman* **and click Add.**

3. **Create a custom property to specify that the document has been approved for printing.**

   a. In the Name text box, **type *Approved For Printing***

   b. From the Type drop-down list, **select Yes Or No.**

   c. **Verify that Yes is selected in the Value section and then click Add.**

   d. In the Properties section, notice that the two custom properties are listed.

   e. **Click OK** to close the Completed Annual Report.docx Properties dialog box.

   f. **Save the document as *My Completed Annual Report.docx* and close it.**

   g. **Close the Document Information panel.**

TOPIC B
Hide Text

In today's business environment, preventing proprietary or personal data from becoming public is very important. One of the best ways to keep information private is to hide it. In this topic, you will hide text.

Your coworker has asked you to help him collect information about the history of the company for a presentation. Documentation on this is available, but it contains certain details about the company that it is critical remain private. You hide the content that you don't want him to view and send the document.

How to Hide Text

Procedure Reference: Hide Text in a Document

To hide text in a document:

1. If necessary, show the non-printing characters.
    - On the Home tab, in the Paragraph group, click the Show/Hide button.
    - Or, show the non-printing characters using the Word Options dialog box.
        a. Display the Word Options dialog box.
        b. In the left pane, select the Display category.
        c. In the Always Show These Formatting Marks On The Screen section, check the Show All Formatting Marks check box, and click OK.
2. Select the text to be hidden.
3. On the Home tab, in the Font group, click the Dialog Box Launcher button to display the Font dialog box.
4. In the Effects section, check the Hidden check box and click OK.
5. If necessary, print the hidden text.
    a. Display the Display category in the Word Options dialog box.
    b. In the Printing Options section, check the Print Hidden Text check box, and click OK.
    c. Click the Office button and choose Print→Print.
    d. In the Print dialog box, specify the desired options, and click OK.

Procedure Reference: Find Hidden Text

To find hidden text:

1. On the Home tab, in the Editing group, click Find.
2. In the Find And Replace dialog box, click More.
3. Click Format and choose Font to display the Find Font dialog box.
4. In the Effects section, check the Hidden check box and click OK.
5. If necessary, click Find Next to locate any other piece of hidden text.
6. If necessary, in the Microsoft Office Word message box, click OK.
7. Close the Find And Replace dialog box.

ACTIVITY 6-2

Hiding Text in a Document

Data Files:

Stockholder Insert.docx

Before You Begin:

From the C:\084895Data\Securing a Document folder, open Stockholder Insert.docx.

Scenario:

The company's marketing manager wants to create a document from the annual report's To Our Stockholders section. He wants the document to include the Milestones section as well as the Strategy text and chart. He especially wants the company's legal issues to be hidden from potential clients.

What You Do	How You Do It
1. **Hide the "To Our Stockholders" heading.**	a. **Select the To Our Stockholders heading.**
	b. On the Home tab, in the Font group, **click the Dialog Box Launcher button** to display the Font dialog box.
	c. In the Effects section, **check the Hidden check box and click OK.**
2. **Hide the "Legal Issues" paragraph.**	a. **Scroll down and select the "Legal Issues" heading and the two paragraphs below it.**
	b. **Display the Font dialog box, check the Hidden check box, and click OK.**
	c. In the Paragraph group, **click the Show/ Hide button.**
	d. Notice that only the Milestones and Strategy sections are shown.
	e. **Save the document as *My Stockholder Insert.docx* and close it.**

TOPIC C

Remove Personal Information from a Document

You know to hide information in a document. However, hiding content may not prevent others from viewing it. In this topic, you will remove personal information from a document.

Even though you haven't worked in the Sales division for over two years, you are still getting phone calls from sales representatives asking if you have updated the sales training document. You wonder why they keep calling you. Then, you find out it's because you originally created the document and your name is still in the Author field of the document's properties. If you had saved the document without your personal information, you could have avoided these calls.

The Document Inspector Dialog Box

The Document Inspector dialog box provides you with various options to identify specific content in a document.

The following table describes the options in the Document Inspector dialog box.

Option	*Summary of the Function It Performs*
Comments, Revisions, Versions, And Annotations	Inspects the document for comments, versions, revision marks and ink annotations.
Document Properties And Personal Information	Inspects for hidden metadata and personal information saved in a document.
Custom XML Data	Inspects for custom XML data stored with a document.
Headers, Footers, And Watermarks	Inspects the document for information on the header, footer, and watermark.
Hidden Text	Inspects the document for text that has been formatted as hidden.

How to Remove Personal Information from a Document

Procedure Reference: Delete Custom Properties

To delete custom properties:

1. Display the document Properties dialog box.

2. Select the Custom tab.

3. In the Properties list box, select the custom property you want to remove and click Delete.

4. Click OK to close the dialog box.

Procedure Reference: Remove Personal Information Using the Document Inspector

To remove personal information using the Document Inspector:

1. If necessary, open the document from which you want to remove the personal information.

2. Click the Office button and choose Prepare→Inspect Document.

3. In the Document Inspector dialog box, check the Document Properties And Personal Information check box and click Inspect.

4. Review the results of the inspection.

5. If necessary, next to the inspection results, click Remove All to remove the document properties and personal information from the document.

6. Click Close.

ACTIVITY 6-3

Removing Personal Information from a Document

Data Files:

My Completed Annual Report.docx

Before You Begin:

From the C:\084895Data\Securing a Document folder, open My Completed Annual Report.docx.

Scenario:

You are ready to send the annual report document for printing. However, before you email the document to the printing house, you need to ensure that it is devoid of personal information.

What You Do	How You Do It
1. Remove the custom value specified for the Editor property.	a. **Display the Document Information panel.**
	b. **Display the document Properties dialog box.**
	c. On the Custom tab, in the Properties list box, **select the Editor property with the Value of Mary Coleman.**
	d. **Click Delete and then click OK.**
	e. **Save the document as** *My Annual Report.docx*
2. Remove all personal information using the Document Inspector.	a. **Click the Office button and choose Prepare→Inspect Document.**
	b. **Uncheck all the check boxes other than the Document Properties And Personal Information check box and click Inspect.**
	c. **Click Remove All** to remove all personal information from your document and **click Close.**
	d. **Save and close the document.**

TOPIC D
Set Formatting and Editing Restrictions

You know how to remove personal information from a document. But, sometimes that measure alone is not enough to protect your documents. To preserve the authenticity of your document you will need to prevent others from changing its content. In this topic, you will specify formatting and editing restrictions for a given document.

You want your reviewers to focus on the content of your document, not its formatting. Before sending the document for review, you can limit their ability to format the document. This way you can prevent them from trying to modify how something is formatted and keep them focused on the task at hand. It also ensures that you won't have to undo any formatting changes they might have made.

The Restrict Formatting And Editing Task Pane

The Restrict Formatting And Editing task pane is used to apply formatting and editing restrictions to a document. It consists of three sections.

The following table describes the sections in the Restrict Formatting And Editing task pane.

Section	Description
Formatting Restrictions	Limits formatting to the set of styles specified in the Formatting Restrictions dialog box.
Editing Restrictions	Restricts the type of editing that can be performed in a document.
Start Enforcement	Allows you to enforce the restrictions on the document specified in the Restrict Formatting And Editing task pane.

Editing Restrictions

There are four types of editing restrictions that can be enforced on a document.

Type	Description
Tracked Changes	Forces change tracking to be enabled.
Comments	Allows only comments to be added to the protected document.
Filling In Forms	Allows only information to be entered in form fields.
No Changes (Read Only)	Prevents any changes from being made to the document.

How to Set Formatting and Editing Restrictions

Procedure Reference: Limit Formatting Choices in a Document

To limit formatting choices in a document:

1. Display the Restrict Formatting And Editing task pane.

   - Display the Restrict Formatting And Editing task pane using the Ribbon.

     a. On the Developer tab, in the Protect group, click Protect Document, or on the Review tab, in the Protect group, click Protect Document.

     b. Choose Restrict Formatting And Editing.

   - Or, display the Restrict Formatting And Editing task pane using the Save As dialog box.

     a. Click the Office button and choose Save As.

     b. In the Save As dialog box, click Tools and choose General Options.

     c. In the General Options dialog box, click Protect Document.

     d. Close the Save As dialog box.

2. In the Formatting Restrictions section, check the Limit Formatting To A Selection Of Styles check box.

3. Click the Settings link.

4. In the Checked Styles Are Currently Allowed list box, uncheck the styles you want to prevent from being used and click OK.

5. In the Microsoft Office Word message box, click Yes.

6. In the Restrict Formatting And Editing task pane, in the Start Enforcement section, click Yes, Start Enforcing Protection.

7. If necessary, in the Start Enforcing Protection dialog box, enter and reenter the password to enforce the formatting restriction and click OK.

Procedure Reference: Specify Editing Restrictions for a Document

To specify editing restrictions for a document:

1. Display the Restrict Formatting And Editing task pane.

2. If necessary, click Stop Protection.

3. In the Editing Restrictions section, check the Allow Only This Type Of Editing In The Document check box.

4. From the Editing Restrictions drop-down list, select the desired type of editing to allow.

5. If necessary, in the Exceptions (Optional) section, add new groups.

   a. Click the More Users link.

   b. In the Add Users dialog box, in the Enter User Names, Separated By Semicolons text box, type the users' names to be added separated by semicolons.

   c. Click OK.

6. Select the content for which the editing restriction is to be applied.

7. If necessary, in the Groups list box, check the desired group to allow the editing restriction specified for the selected content to be applied to that group.

8. If necessary, in the Individuals list box, check the desired individuals to allow the editing restriction specified for the selected content to be applied to those individuals.

When you select more than one individual, the individuals are grouped together and are listed in the Groups list box.

9. In the Start Enforcement section, click Yes, Start Enforcing Protection.

10. In the Start Enforcing Protection dialog box, click OK.

11. If necessary, click Find Next Region I Can Edit to navigate to the next region that can be edited.

12. If necessary, click Show All Regions I Can Edit to highlight all regions that can be edited.

13. If necessary, click in a region that can be edited and apply editing restrictions to it.

14. If necessary, remove the formatting and editing restrictions.

    a. In the Restrict Formatting And Editing task pane, click Stop Protection.

    b. If necessary, in the Unprotect Document dialog box, in the Password text box, type the password and click OK.

    c. In the Editing Restrictions section, uncheck the Allow Only This Type Of Editing In The Document check box and click Yes to remove the ignored exceptions.

    d. Uncheck the Limit Formatting To A Selection Of Styles check box.

ACTIVITY 6-4
Setting Formatting and Editing Restrictions

Data Files:

Financial Highlights.docx

Before You Begin:

1. From the C:\084895Data\Securing a Document folder, open Financial Highlights.docx.

2. In the Word Options dialog box, in the Popular category, check the Show Developer Tab In The Ribbon check box, and then click OK.

3. Close the Document Information panel.

Scenario:

You want your coworkers to provide ideas for the financial highlights document. However, you don't want them to modify content in the document.

What You Do	How You Do It
1. **Apply editing restrictions to the document.**	a. On the Developer tab, in the Protect group, **click Protect Document and choose Restrict Formatting And Editing.**
	b. In the Restrict Formatting And Editing task pane, in the Editing Restrictions section, **check the Allow Only This Type Of Editing In The Document check box.**
	c. In the Editing Restrictions drop-down list, **verify that No Changes (Read Only) is selected.**
2. **Enforce the editing restrictions.**	a. In the Start Enforcement section, **click Yes, Start Enforcing Protection.**
	b. In the Start Enforcing Protection dialog box, **click OK.**
	c. In the Restrict Formatting And Editing task pane, in the Your Permissions section, notice the message displayed. **Close the Restrict Formatting And Editing task pane.**
	d. **Save the document as *My Financial Highlights.docx* and close it.**

TOPIC E

Add a Digital Signature to a Document

You know how to prevent formatting and editing changes to your document. Another security concern is the ability to verify that a document is from the intended source and contains the original content. In this topic, you will add a digital signature to a document.

You've been receiving an uncommon number of expense reports from a particular sales person. When you call her, she denies ever sending the ones in question. Someone else has been submitting the extra reports using her computer and cashing the extra reimbursement checks. This could have been prevented if you could have checked the authenticity of the reports.

Digital Signature

Definition:

A *digital signature* is an electronic signature that can be used to identify an individual. When you attach a digital signature to a document, the document is considered to be signed. Once signed, the document cannot be modified without removing the digital signature. It can be both visible and invisible.

Example:

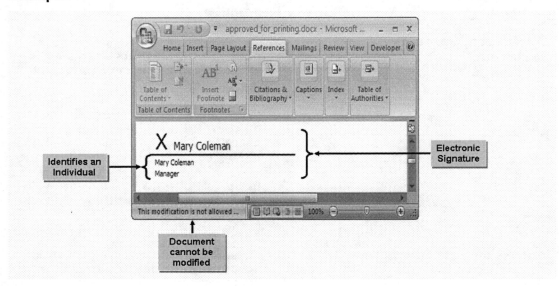

The Signature Line

A *signature line* is used to add a digital signature to a document. A signature line is usually found at the end of the document, though it can be used anywhere in the document. It records the content exactly as it is when it is signed and it also allows the signature to be verified when needed. You can add either text or images to a signature line.

The Signatures Task Pane

The *Signatures task pane* lists all of the signatures in a document. It groups the signatures based on their category. There are two categories of signatures: Valid Signatures and Requested Signatures. Valid Signatures include all the information and the signature details. The Requested Signatures include only the signature setup information.

Requested Signatures

Requested Signatures are signatures that contain the setup information required for creating a signature. This could include information such as the signer's name, title, email address, and other instructions for the signer.

Valid Signatures

Valid Signatures are signatures that contain signature details in addition to the signature setup information. In addition to the signer's name, title, email address and other instructions, Valid Signatures also contain the text or image used to sign a document digitally.

How to Add a Digital Signature to a Document

Procedure Reference: Create a Digital ID

To create a digital ID:

1. On the Insert tab, in the Text group, click the Signature Line button drop-down arrow and choose Microsoft Office Signature Line.
2. In the Microsoft Office Word dialog box, click OK.
3. In the Signature Setup dialog box, specify the desired options.
    a. In the Suggested Signer text box, type a name.
    b. In the Suggested Signer's Title text box, type a designation.
    c. In the Suggested Signer's E-mail Address text box, type an email address.
    d. If necessary, in the Instructions To The Signer text box, type the desired instructions.
    e. Check the Allow The Signer To Add Comments In The Sign Dialog check box to allow comments to be added along with the signature.
    f. Check the Show Sign Date In Signature Line check box to show the date when the signature is added in the signature line.
4. Click OK.

Procedure Reference: Sign a Document

To sign a document:

1. Double-click the digital ID.
2. In the Microsoft Office Word dialog box, click OK.
3. In the Sign dialog box, specify the appropriate options.
    - In the X text box, type your name to add a printed version of your signature.

Tablet PC users can sign their names in the text box next to the X by using the inking feature to add a handwritten signature.

- Or, click Select Image, navigate to and select the desired image, and click Select to select an image of the written signature.

4. Click Sign, and in the Signature Confirmation dialog box, click OK.

5. If necessary, remove the digital signature.

    a. Display the Signatures task pane.

        - In the status bar, click the red ribbon icon.

        - Or, click the Office button and choose Prepare→View Signatures.

    b. Remove the signature.

        - In the Valid Signatures list box, select the signature, click the signature's drop-down arrow and choose Remove Signature.

        - Or, right-click the digital signature and choose Remove Signature.

    c. In the Remove Signature dialog box, click Yes.

    d. In the Signature Removed dialog box, click OK.

ACTIVITY 6-5

Adding a Digital Signature to a Document

Data Files:

Approved For Printing.docx

Before You Begin:

From the C:\084895Data\Securing a Document folder, open Approved For Printing.docx.

Scenario:

Your commercial printer has notified you that another person in your company has been sending print jobs to them using your name. As a result, your department is being billed for unapproved work. You need to avoid the reoccurrence of such incidents.

What You Do	How You Do It
1. Create a digital ID.	a. **Place your cursor at the end of the document.**
	b. On the Insert tab, in the Text group, **click the Signature Line button drop-down arrow and choose Microsoft Office Signature Line.**
	c. In the Microsoft Office Word dialog box, **click OK.**
	d. In the Signature Setup dialog box, in the Suggested Signer text box, **type your name** and in the Suggested Signer's Title text box, **type your designation.**
	e. In the Suggested Signer's E-mail Address text box, **type your email address and click OK** to add the digital signature.
2. Sign the document.	a. **Double-click the digital ID** and in the Microsoft Office Word dialog box, **click OK.**
	b. In the Sign dialog box, in the X text box, **type your name and click Sign.**
	c. In the Signature Confirmation dialog box, **click OK** to display the signature.
	d. **Close the document.**

TOPIC F
Set a Password for a Document

So far, you have learned how to prevent information from being modified. You can also prevent unauthorized users from opening a document. In this topic, you will set a password for a document.

You just got a call from your contact at the advertising agency your company uses. She said that the document you sent them is password protected and they need the password before they can write the press release. A quick check tells you that you sent the wrong document with some sensitive information in it. But, because you had password protected the document, no harm was done.

How to Set Password for a Document

Procedure Reference: Set a Password for a Document

To set a password for a document:

1. Click the Office button and choose Save As.
2. In the Save As dialog box, click Tools and choose General Options.
3. In the General Options dialog box, in the Password To Open text box, type the password and click OK.
4. In the Confirm Password dialog box, in the Reenter Password To Open text box, retype the password and click OK.
5. Save the document to set the password.
6. If necessary, verify that the document has been password protected.
    a. Close the password-protected document.
    b. Reopen the password-protected document.
    c. In the Password dialog box, in the Enter Password To Open File text box, type the correct password.
    d. Click OK to open the document.
7. If desired, remove the password.
    a. Display the General Options dialog box, delete the password, and click OK.
    b. Save the document to remove the password.

Password Tips

Passwords are case sensitive and can include up to 15 letters, numbers, punctuation, spaces, and symbols. By mixing a variety of cases and characters, you can make the password difficult to guess. However, you also need to ensure that your password is memorable because if you forget it, you will have difficulties opening the document.

ACTIVITY 6-6

Setting a Password for a Document

Data Files:

Salary Review.docx

Before You Begin:

From the C:\084895Data\Securing a Document folder, open Salary Review.docx.

Scenario:

The Salary Review document contains some sensitive information regarding whether or not certain employees can be approved for raises. You want to make sure that only authorized people are able to open the document.

What You Do	How You Do It
1. Password protect the document.	a. **Click the Office button and choose Save As.**
	b. In the Save As dialog box, **click Tools and choose General Options.**
	c. In the General Options dialog box, in the Password To Open text box, **type *password* and click OK.**
	d. In the Confirm Password dialog box, in the Reenter Password To Open text box, **type *password* and click OK.**
	e. **Save the document as *My Salary Review.docx* and close it.**
2. Verify that the document has been password protected.	a. **Open My Salary Review.docx from the C:\084895Data\Securing a Document folder.**
	b. In the Password dialog box, in the Enter Password To Open File text box, **type *password* and click OK.**
	c. Observe that My Salary Review.docx opens.
	d. **Close My Salary Review.docx** without saving any changes.

TOPIC G
Restrict Document Access

In the previous topic, you learned how to password protect a document. Applying levels of permission is another way to control access to your documents. In this topic, you will restrict access to a document.

In the course of your work, you may need to prevent sensitive information from being reused in any form, be it hard copy or electronic. By setting levels of permission, you can restrict the usage of the contents in a document.

Access Levels

Access levels determine the permission granted to a user to manipulate the content in a document.

The following table describes the access levels in a document.

Level	Description
Read	Only allows the user to read a document.
Change	Allows the user to read, edit, and save changes to a document.
Full Control	Allows the user to read, edit, save changes, and print a document.

The Mark As Final Option

The Mark As Final option can be used to imply to readers that the document sent to them is the final version. When you set the Mark As Final option for a document, the document is saved in the read-only mode. When a reader opens the document in Word 2007, all editing tools are disabled and the Mark As Final icon is displayed on the Microsoft Office Status Bar. A reader can change the status and edit the document by deselecting the Mark As Final option.

 When you open a document that is marked as final in earlier versions of Word, it does not open in the read-only mode. All editing tools will be accessible.

How to Restrict Document Access

Procedure Reference: Restrict Access to Content in a Document

To restrict access to content in a document:

1. Click the Office button and choose Prepare→Restrict Permission→Restricted Access.
2. In the Permission dialog box, check the Restrict Permission To This Document check box.
3. In the Choose Profile dialog box, click OK.
4. In the Read or Change text box, enter the email addresses of specific users, as desired.
5. Click More Options and in the The Following Users Have Permission To This Document list box, select the desired user.
6. From the Access Level drop-down list for that user, select the desired access level.
7. If necessary, set an expiration date for a document.
    a. In the Additional Permissions For Users section, check the This Document Expires On check box.
    b. Click the This Document Expires On drop-down arrow, and using the date picker, select a date.
8. Click OK to exit the Permission dialog box.

Procedure Reference: Mark a Document as Final

To mark a document as final:

1. Click the Office button and choose Prepare→Mark As Final.
2. In the warning box that indicates that the document will be marked as final and saved, click OK.
3. In the message box that indicates that the document has been marked as final, click OK.

DISCOVERY ACTIVITY 6-7

Restricting Document Access

Data Files:

Restricting Access_guided.exe

Setup:

This is a simulated activity. In this simulation, you are Mary Coleman and your email address is mcoleman@xchg.com. The Microsoft Rights Management Services is available on your network.

Scenario:

You need to mail a document that contains vital information about your company's strategies, and with security being a major concern, you decide to assign permission levels to restrict unauthorized users from accessing the document. You also need to make sure that the document is not accessed after a specific time by any users.

---

1. To launch the simulation, **browse to the C:\084895Data\Securing a Document\ Simulations folder.**

2. **Double-click the Restricting Access_guided.exe file.**

3. **Maximize the simulation window.**

4. **Follow the on-screen steps for the simulation.**

5. When you have finished the activity, **close the simulation window.**

Lesson 6 Follow-up

In this lesson, you improved the security of a document by updating document properties with accurate personal information and protecting them from unwanted changes by setting formatting and editing restrictions. You then added a digital signature and a password to the document. You can use one or more of these security methods in order to secure your own documents.

1. **What security measures do you currently use to protect your documents?**

2. **What new security measures do you plan to use to protect your documents?**

Follow-up

In this course, you created, managed, revised, and distributed long documents and forms. You discovered how Word can be used with other programs for document collaboration, and made documents and information accessible to specific people and programs.

1.   **How will you use other programs to enhance Word's functionality?**

2.   **In Word, what collaboration tools will you use to manage, revise, and distribute documents?**

3.   **What are the advantages of maintaining different versions of a document in your organization?**

What's Next?

This is the last course in the series.

Creating Forms

Lesson Time: 1 hour(s), 25 minutes

Objectives:

In this lesson, you will create forms.

You will:

- Add form fields to a document.
- Protect a form.
- Save form data as plain text.
- Automate a form.

Introduction

During the course of a workday, you may need to collect some information from customers or coworkers. In this lesson, you will create forms so that you can collect the desired information in a consistent and efficient manner.

Every day you get dozens of phone calls from people wanting to be added to your company's mailing list. To fulfill a request, you need to obtain the same information from each person: the person's name, address, and the lists he or she wants to join. In Microsoft® Office Word 2007, you can create forms to help you consistently capture such information.

TOPIC A

Add Form Fields to a Document

You have created documents to present information either on a computer screen or in print. Documents can also be used to collect information in a consistent format. In this topic, you will add form fields to a document.

As you were checking numbers in a Microsoft® Office Excel® worksheet, a potential client called asking you to mail the company's latest marketing material to him. You quickly scribble down the person's name and street address, but you forget to ask for city, state, and postal code information. If you had a form containing fields for you to enter all of those necessary details, you may not have forgotten to ask for the information.

Forms

Definition:

A *form* is a document used to collect information for a particular purpose in a consistent format. Whether forms are paper-based or electronic, they contain boilerplate text such as the form title, labels, and fields. Users can enter information in these fields, but they will not be able to alter the form.

Example:

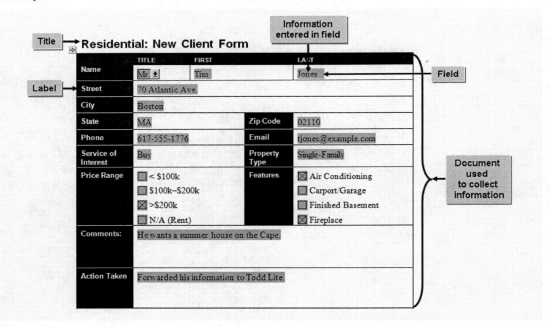

Plan a Form

Before you begin creating a form in Word, you should decide what information you want to capture and where you want that information to appear in the form. You also need to consider how the form will be distributed and whether or not you want to protect the form. When you begin creating the form, consider using a table to contain the various form fields. Tables allow you to control the form's layout with more precision.

Using an existing paper form or diagramming a new form on paper is a useful way to plan a form. By experimenting with paper diagrams, you can save time when you start inserting form fields.

Form Fields

Definition:

A *form field* is a container inserted into a form that is used to collect a specific type of information. Each form field has a name signifying the type of entry it requires. Form fields also have their own set of options. These options can be used to determine the type and format of the data that the user is allowed to enter in that field and how the user input is captured.

Example:

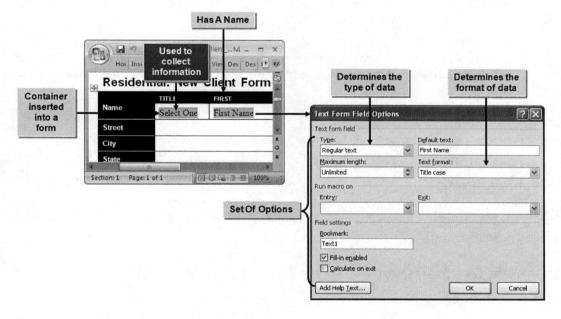

Types of Form Fields

Each form field can be used to collect a particular type of data. There are three types of form fields.

Form Field	Description
Text	Used to collect textual, numeric, or date-related information.
Check Box	Used to allow users to select several answers from several choices.
Drop-Down	Used to allow users to select a single answer from several choices.

Form Field Options

The form field options vary based on the type of form field selected.

Form Field	Options Include
Text	Type of data that can be entered; default text to be displayed; maximum field length; text, number, and date formats; macro handling; bookmark names; and help text options.
Check Box	Check box size; default value; macro handling; bookmark names; and help text options.
Drop-Down	Drop-down items; item order; macro handling; bookmark names; and help text options.

Legacy Tools

The Legacy Tools menu contains options to add form fields and ActiveX controls to a document. It can be accessed on the Developer tab, in the Controls group.

ActiveX Controls

ActiveX Controls are software components that can be used to perform specific tasks. You can run ActiveX Controls from within the Word application. ActiveX Controls have access to the complete Windows operating system.

Content Controls

Content controls are controls that can be added to forms, templates, and documents. They can be designed to collect a specific type of information.

The Controls Group

The Controls group contains content controls and form fields which you can use to design forms. It also contains the Properties button that is used to display the properties of a form field or a content control.

How to Add Form Fields to a Document

Procedure Reference: Add a Drop-Down Form Field

To add a drop-down form field:

1. If necessary, display the Developer tab on the Ribbon.
    a. Display the Word Options dialog box.
    b. In the right pane, in the Top Options For Working With Word section, check the Show Developer Tab In The Ribbon check box and click OK.
2. Place the insertion point where you want to insert the drop-down form field.
3. On the Developer tab, in the Controls group, click Legacy Tools and then, in the Legacy Forms section, select Drop-Down Form Field.
4. In the Controls group, click Properties.

5. In the Drop-Down Form Field Options dialog box, set the drop-down form field's options.

   a. In the Drop-Down Item text box, type the name of a list item.

   b. Click Add to add the item to the list.

   c. If necessary, add more list items.

   d. If necessary, select a list item and click the appropriate button to move the item up or down until the item is in the desired position.

   e. If necessary, select an item and click Remove to remove the item.

6. Click OK to insert the drop-down form field.

 To display a field's properties, double-click the form field or right-click the form field and choose Properties.

 After you create a form field, you will need to protect the form before the fields will work as intended.

Procedure Reference: Add a Text Form Field

To add a text form field:

1. Place the insertion point where you want to insert the text form field.

2. In the Controls group, click Legacy Tools and then, in the Legacy Forms section, select Text Form Field.

3. Click Properties.

4. If necessary, in the Text Form Field Options dialog box, set the text form field's options.

   a. From the Type drop-down list, select the type of information that will be entered in the form field.

      - Regular Text: Use when the form field will contain basic text.

      - Number: Use when the form field will contain numbers that you want formatted in a particular way.

      - Date: Use when the form field will contain a date.

      - Current Date: Use when the form field should contain the current date.

      - Current Time: Use when the form field should contain the current time.

      - Calculation: Use when the form field should contain a mathematical calculation.

   b. In the Default Text text box, type the default information that will be initially displayed in the form field.

 Depending on the type you select, the Default text box may also display the default number, default date, or default expression.

    c.   In the Maximum Length spin box, set the desired number of characters that can be entered in the form field.

    d.   From the Text Format drop-down list, select the desired format.

 Depending on the type you select, the Text Format drop-down list may also display the Number Format, Date Format, or Time Format.

5.   Click OK to insert the text form field.

Procedure Reference: Add a Check Box Form Field

To add a check box form field:

1.   Place the insertion point where you want to insert the check box form field.

2.   In the Controls group, click Legacy Tools and then, in the Legacy Forms section, select Check Box Form Field to insert the check box form field.

3.   Click Properties.

4.   If necessary, in the Check Box Form Field Options dialog box, set the check box form field options.

    a.   Set the size of the check box.

- Set the check box size to Auto.
- Or, set the check box size to an exact size.

    b.   Set the default value of the check box.

- In the Default Value section, select the Not Checked option to set the default value of the check box as unchecked.
- Or, in the Default Value Section, select the Checked option to set the default value of the check box as checked.

5.   Click OK to insert the check box form field.

6.   Press the Spacebar and type the text that will act as the label for the check box.

ACTIVITY A-1

Adding Form Fields to a Document

Data Files:

New Client Form.docx

Before You Begin:

From the C:\084895Data\Appendix A folder, open New Client Form.docx.

Scenario:

You have been asked to contribute to a new form that will eventually be a template used by Burke Properties customer service representatives to capture information from new clients interested in the company's residential services.

What You Do	How You Do It
1. Insert a drop-down form field that lists all Title items.	a. On the Ribbon, **choose the Developer tab.**
	b. In the form, in the table cell below Title, **click to place the insertion point.**
	c. In the Controls group, **click the Legacy Tools button** and then, in the Legacy Forms section, **select Drop-Down Form Field.**
	d. **Click Properties.**
	e. In the Drop-Down Form Field Options dialog box, in the Drop-Down Item text box, **type *Dr.* and click Add.**
	f. **Similarly, add *Miss, Mr., Mrs., Ms.,* and *Select One* as list items.**
	g. **Click the Move down arrow button** to move the Select One item to the top of the drop-down list and **click OK.**

2. Insert text form fields for the client's first and last names.

   a. In the empty table cell below First, **click to place the insertion point.**

   b. In the Controls group, **click Legacy Tools and select Text Form Field.** `ab|`

   c. **Click Properties.**

   d. In the Text Form Field Options dialog box, in the Default Text text box, **type *First Name***

   e. From the Text Format drop-down list, **select Title Case and click OK.**

   f. In the empty cell below Last, **insert a text form field with the default text *Last Name***

   g. From the Text Format drop-down list, **select Title Case and click OK.**

---

3. Insert a text form field for the zip code.

   a. In the empty cell to the right of the Zip Code, **click to place the insertion point.**

   b. **Insert a text form field and display the Text Form Field Options dialog box.**

   c. In the Text Form Field section, from the Type drop-down list, **select Number.**

   d. In the Maximum Length spin box, **double-click and type *5***

   e. In the Number Format text box, **type ##### and click OK.**

4. **Insert check box form fields for the price range.**

   a. In the empty cell to the right of Price Range, **click to place the insertion point.**

   b. In the Controls group, **click Legacy Tools** and then, in the Legacy Forms section, **select Check Box Form Field.** ☑

   c. **Press the Spacebar, type** *<$100k* **and press Enter.**

   d. **Insert a second check box form field with the label** *$100k-$200k* **and press Enter.**

   e. **Insert another two check box form fields with the labels** *>$200k* **and** *N/A (Rent)*

5. **Insert text form fields for the client's contact information, comments, and actions taken.**

   a. In the empty table cell to the right of Street, **insert a text form field with the default text** *Street Name*

   b. In the empty table cell to the right of City, **insert a text form field with the label** *City Name*

   c. In the empty table cell to the right of Phone, **insert a text form field for the Phone field so that it accepts numbers in the format ###-###-####**

   d. In the empty table cell to the right of Email, **insert a text form field for the email address.**

   e. In the empty table cell to the right of Comments, **insert a text form field with the label** *Enter Comments Here* **and set the Text Format property as First Capital.**

   f. In the empty table cell to the right of Action Taken, **insert a text form field with the label** *Enter Actions Taken Here* **and set the Text Format property as First Capital.**

6. **Insert drop-down form fields containing list items for the State, Service of Interest, and Property Type fields.**

 a. In the empty table cell to the right of State, **insert a drop-down form field with the following items:** *Select One, CA, FL, LA, KY, MA, MD, OH,* **and** *TX*

 b. In the empty table cell to the right of Service Of Interest, **insert a drop-down form field with the following items:** *Select One, Buy, Rent/Sublet,* **and** *Sell*

 c. In the empty table cell to the right of Property Type, **insert a drop-down form field with the following items:** *Select One, Apartment, Condo/Town House, Multi-Family,* **and** *Single-Family*

7. **Insert check box form fields for the Features field.**

 a. In the empty table cell to the right of Features, **insert a check box form field with the label** *Air Conditioning*

 b. **Similarly, add the following check box form fields below the Air Conditioning check box:** *Carport/Garage, Finished Basement,* **and** *Fireplace*

 c. **Save the document as** *My New Client Form.docx* **and close it.**

TOPIC B
Protect a Form

You have added form fields to a document. Now, you may want to ensure that only the form fields can be filled in and that the form's other contents cannot be altered. In this topic, you will protect a form.

After spending hours creating an expense form that contains all of the information you need to gather, you email it to the sales people so that they can begin using it. As the expense forms are returned to you, you notice that many of the sales people modified the form to suit their needs. Protecting the form would have prevented them from making changes to the form.

How to Protect a Form
Procedure Reference: Password Protect a Completed Form

To password protect a completed form:

1. On the Developer tab, in the Protect group, click Protect Document and choose Restrict Formatting And Editing.
2. In the Restrict Formatting And Editing task pane, in the Editing Restrictions section, check the Allow Only This Type Of Editing In The Document check box.
3. Below the check box, from the drop-down list, select Filling In Forms.
4. In the Start Enforcement section, click Yes, Start Enforcing Protection.
5. In the Start Enforcing Protection dialog box, in the Enter New Password (Optional) text box, type the desired password and press Tab.
6. In the Reenter Password To Confirm text box, retype the password and click OK to protect the form.
7. If necessary, remove password protection from the form.
   a. If necessary, display the Restrict Formatting And Editing task pane.
   b. Click Stop Protection.
   c. In the Unprotect Document dialog box, in the Password text box, type the password and click OK to unprotect the form.

Form Field Shading Button
The Form Field Shading button is used to give a shading effect to the form field. It makes the field visible to the person developing the form.

Locked Forms
When a form is locked, only the Form Field Shading buttons are enabled. Additionally, only the form fields themselves can be modified. Boilerplate text, page set up, and other formatting options are unavailable.

Procedure Reference: Add Custom Help to a Text Form Field

To add custom help to a form field:
1. Select the desired form field.
2. In the Controls group, click Properties.
3. In the Text Form Field Options dialog box, click Add Help Text.

4. In the Form Field Help Text dialog box, on the Status Bar tab, click in the Type Your Own text box and type the desired text.

5. Click OK to add the custom help text to the text form field.

Using Additional Help Text

If you need to provide a longer description than can be displayed on the status bar, you can type a longer help description in the Type Your Own text box on the Help Key (F1) tab. Both the status bar and the Help key can be used together. To display the Help key text, select the appropriate form field and press F1.

Procedure Reference: Reset Form Fields

To reset form fields:

1. On the Ribbon, select the Developer tab.

2. In the Controls group, click the Legacy Tools button and then, in the Legacy Forms section, select Reset Form Fields.

ACTIVITY A-2

Protecting a Form

Before You Begin:

My New Client Form.docx is open.

Scenario:

The form that Burke Properties customer service representatives will use to capture information from new clients interested in the company's residential services is nearly done. All that remains is to password protect the form, test the form and modify the form fields, as needed. When you finish testing the form, you want to make sure that the form is password protected again, before saving it as a template.

What You Do	How You Do It
1. Password protect the form allowing users to only fill in the form fields.	a. On the Developer tab, in the Protect group, **click Protect Document and choose Restrict Formatting And Editing.**
	b. In the Restrict Formatting And Editing task pane, in the Editing Restrictions section, **check the Allow Only This Type Of Editing In The Document check box.**
	c. In the Editing Restrictions section, from the drop-down list, **select Filling In Forms.**
	d. In the Start Enforcement section, **click Yes, Start Enforcing Protection.**
	e. In the Start Enforcing Protection dialog box, in the Enter New Password (Optional) text box, **type *password* and press Tab.**
	f. In the Reenter Password To Confirm text box, **type *password* and click OK.**

2. **Test the form by entering some sample information.**

   a. In the form, from the Title drop-down list, **select Ms.**

   b. **Press Tab** to move to the next field, and type *Sue*

   c. **Press Tab and type** *Smith*

   d. **Press Tab and type** *1 Elm Dr.*

   e. **Press Tab and type** *Akron*

   f. **Press Tab** and from the State drop-down list, **select OH.**

   g. **Press Tab and type** *44305*

   h. **Press Tab and type** *555-6560*

   i. **Fill in the listed information in the appropriate form fields:**

- Email: *ssmith@example.com*
- Service of Interest: *Buy*
- Property Type: *Single-family*
- Price Range: *$100k-$200k*
- Features: *Air Conditioning, Carport/Garage*

3. **Unprotect the form and add help text prompting the user to enter the area code.**

   a. In the Restrict Formatting And Editing task pane, **click Stop Protection.**

   b. In the Unprotect Document dialog box, in the Password text box, **type** *password* **and click OK.**

   c. Next to the Phone label, **double-click the text form field** to display its properties.

   d. In the Text Form Field Options dialog box, **click Add Help Text.**

   e. In the Form Field Help Text dialog box, on the Status Bar tab, **click in the Type Your Own text box, and type** *Include the area code.* **Click OK.**

   f. In the Text Form Field Options dialog box, **click OK.**

4. **Protect the form and test whether the help text is displayed for Phone form field.**

a. In the Restrict Formatting And Editing task pane, in the Start Enforcement section, **click Yes, Start Enforcing Protection.**

b. In the Start Enforcing Protection dialog box, in the Enter New Password (Optional) text box, **type *password* and press Tab.**

c. In the Reenter Password To Confirm text box, **type *password* and click OK.**

d. **Press Tab** to deselect the Phone text form field.

e. **Select the Phone text form field** to view the help text displayed in the status bar.

f. In the Phone text form field, **type *330-555-6560***

5. **Save the form as a template.**

a. **Unprotect the form.**

b. In the Controls group, **click the Legacy Tools button** and then in the Legacy Forms section, **select Reset Form Fields** to reset the form fields.

c. **Password protect the form.**

d. **Click the Office button and choose Save As.**

e. From the Save As Type drop-down list, **select Word Template (*.dotx).**

f. In the File Name text box, **select the existing text, type *My Protected New Client Form* and click Save.**

g. **Close the template.**

TOPIC C
Save Form Data as Plain Text

You protected a form to prevent users from altering the content. Although forms can store information, you can also save that information in another file format so that it can be used by other programs. In this topic, you will save form data as a text file.

Whenever you have received 20 expense forms from the sales people, you set aside a day to print the returned forms and key the appropriate information into the payroll database for processing. However, if you save just the form data in a file that can be imported directly into the database, you can save a significant amount of time while avoiding possible data entry errors.

How to Save Form Data as Plain Text

Procedure Reference: Save Form Data as Plain Text

To save form data as plain text:

1. Display the Save As dialog box.
2. Click Tools and choose Save Options.
3. In the Word Options dialog box, in the left pane, select Advanced to display the advanced options in the right pane.
4. In the Preserve Fidelity When Sharing This Document section, check the Save Form Data As Delimited Text File check box.
5. Click OK.
6. If necessary, in the Save As dialog box, in the File Name text box, rename the file.
7. Click Save.
8. In the File Conversion dialog box, observe that the form data is displayed in the Preview list box and then click OK.
9. If necessary, open the form data text file to verify that the data was saved as expected.

Form Data Conversion

When you save form data as plain text, you can generally understand the form field results as they correspond with the order of the form fields in the form itself. Typically, drop-down form fields and text form fields provide logical and understandable results. However, when a check box form field is saved as text, the form field's result is displayed either as a "0" or a "1". A "0" means that the check box was unchecked and a "1" means that the check box was checked.

ACTIVITY A-3
Saving Form Data as Plain Text

Data Files:

Jones Client Form.docx

Before You Begin:

From the C:\084895Data\Appendix A folder, open Jones Client Form.docx.

Scenario:

The company's technology department is experimenting with a new client database that requires information to be saved as text files. The technology department representative wants you to supply him with a sample client form that he can use in his testing.

What You Do	How You Do It
1. Save the data in a form as a plain text file.	a. **Display the Save As dialog box.**
	b. **Click Tools and choose Save Options.**
	c. In the Word Options dialog box, in the left pane, **select Advanced and scroll down to the Preserve Fidelity When Sharing This Document section.**
	d. **Check the Save Form Data As Delimited Text File check box and click OK.**
	e. In the Save As dialog box, in the File Name text box, **select Jones Client Form.txt, type *My Database Sample* and click Save.**
	f. Notice that in the File Conversion - My Database Sample.txt dialog box, the form data is displayed in the Preview list box and **click OK** to save the form data as a text file.

2. **Open the plain text file.**

   a. **Display the Open dialog box.**

   b. From the Files Of Type drop-down list, **select Text Files (.txt).**

   c. **Double-click My Database Sample.txt** to view the form data.

   d. **Close My Database Sample.txt and Jones Client Form.docx without saving changes.**

TOPIC D
Automate a Form

You have saved the data entered in a form's fields as a text file. Forms don't always have to be static data containers. You can automate forms to accomplish a variety of tasks. In this topic, you will automate a form.

The company's realtors want more detailed fields added to the New Homebuyer form to capture more accurate information from the homebuyer. Adding so many fields would make the form very long and not all of the fields would be applicable to each homebuyer. To accommodate the realtors' request, and to keep the form manageable, you automate the form so that when a particular field is selected, additional detailed fields will be displayed.

How to Automate a Form

Procedure Reference: Cross-Reference a Bookmarked Form Field

To cross-reference a bookmarked form field:

1. Prepare form fields to be cross-referenced.
    a. If necessary, unprotect the form.
    b. Display the form field's options.
    c. In the Field Settings section, in the Bookmark text box, type a logical bookmark name.
    d. Check the Calculate On Exit check box and click OK.
2. Place the insertion point where you want to insert the cross-reference.
3. On the References tab, in the Captions group, click Cross-Reference.
4. In the Cross Reference dialog box, from the Reference Type drop-down list, select Bookmark.
5. If necessary, from the Insert Reference To drop-down list, select Bookmark Text.
6. In the For Which Bookmark list box, select the desired bookmark and click Insert.
7. Close the Cross-Reference dialog box.

Usage of Cross-Referencing

When a form field is cross-referenced, the field's results can be displayed elsewhere in the same document. This is especially useful when creating your own form letters.

Field Settings

When a form field is created, it is given a generic bookmark name that describes the type of form field as well as the sequence in which the field was added to the form. For instance, the bookmark name "Dropdown4" identifies the fourth drop-down form field that was inserted into the form. Because a form field contains a bookmark name, the field's results can be cross-referenced. Since a form may contain dozens of similar fields, it is helpful to rename the bookmark so that it will be easier to locate or cross-reference. Additionally, you will want to make sure to check the Calculate On Exit option if you plan on cross-referencing the form field. With this option checked, the cross-reference will be updated automatically when the user exits the form field.

Procedure Reference: Run a Macro from a Form Field

To run a macro from a form field:

1. Display the options for the form field on which you want to run a macro.
2. In the Run Macro On section, from the Entry drop-down list, select the macro you want to run.
3. If necessary, from the Exit drop-down list, select the macro you want to run.
4. Click OK.

 You can run different macros upon entering the field and exiting the field.

Procedure Reference: Print Only the Data From a Form

To print only the data from a form:

1. Display the Print dialog box and click Options.
2. In the Word Options dialog box, in the left pane, select the Advanced category and scroll down.
3. In the When Printing This Document section, check the Print Only The Data From A Form check box and click OK.
4. In the Print dialog box, click OK to print the form data.

 If your company uses preprinted forms, you can design your Word form so that the data from your Word form fills in the corresponding form field on the preprinted form.

ACTIVITY A-4

Automating a Form

Data Files:

Printable New Client Form.dotm

Before You Begin:

1. Open a blank document.

2. Enable macros.

   a. Click the Office button and then choose Word Options.

   b. In the Word Options dialog box, in the left pane, select the Trust Center category.

   c. In the right pane, click Trust Center Settings.

   d. In the right pane, in the Macro Settings section, select Enable All Macros (Not Recommended; Potentially Dangerous Code Can Run) option.

   e. Click OK.

   f. In the Word Options dialog box, click OK.

3. Ensure that the printer and the printer driver are installed on the computer.

4. From the C:\084895Data\Appendix A folder, open Printable New Client Form.dotm.

Scenario:

Whenever a new client's information is taken, a form letter is printed and mailed to that client. The template for that form is nearly finished. You have been asked to automate the template so that the new client's name is automatically entered in the letter where appropriate. You also want to print the form letter by checking the Print Letter check box and test the form once you have made all the changes.

What You Do	How You Do It
1. **Create a bookmark for the Title, First Name, and Last Name form fields.**	a. **Unprotect the form.**

 The password to unprotect the form is *password*

b. In the form, in the cell below the word TITLE, **double-click the drop-down form field.**

c. In the Drop-Down Form Field Options dialog box, in the Field Settings section, in the Bookmark text box, **replace the default text with** *Title*

d. **Check the Calculate On Exit check box and click OK.**

e. In the cell below the word FIRST, **double-click the text form field.**

f. In the Text Form Field Options dialog box, in the Field Settings section, in the Bookmark text box, **replace the default text with** *First*

g. **Check the Calculate On Exit check box and click OK.**

h. In the cell below the word LAST, **double-click the text form field.**

i. In the Text Form Field Options dialog box, in the Field Settings section, in the Bookmark text box, **replace the default text with** *Last*

j. **Check the Calculate On Exit check box and click OK.**

2. **Insert a cross-reference to the Title bookmark.**

a. **Scroll down to the letter** and in the blank line above the Street Name, **click to place the insertion point.**

b. On the References tab, in the Captions group, **click Cross-Reference.**

c. In the Cross-Reference dialog box, from the Reference Type drop-down list, **select Bookmark.**

d. Notice that Bookmark Text is automatically selected in the Insert Reference To drop-down list box.

e. In the For Which Bookmark list box, **scroll down and select Title.**

f. **Click Insert and then click Close.**

3. **Insert cross-references to the First and Last bookmarks.**

 Remember, placing the mouse pointer over a cross-reference will display the name of the reference in a ScreenTip.

a. **Press the Spacebar** and in the Captions group, **click Cross-Reference.**

b. In the Cross-Reference dialog box, in the For Which Bookmark list box, **select First and click Insert.**

c. With the Cross-Reference dialog box open, in the document, after the first name cross-reference, **click to place the insertion point and press the Spacebar.**

d. In the Cross-Reference dialog box, in the For Which Bookmark list box, **select Last and click Insert.**

e. **Click anywhere in the document.**

f. In the document, after the text "Dear" and before the colon, **click to place the insertion point and press the Spacebar.**

g. In the Cross-Reference dialog box, in the For Which Bookmark list box, **select First and click Insert.**

h. **Close the Cross-Reference dialog box.**

4. **Attach the Print Letter macro to the form.**

a. **Scroll up** the document to display the previous page.

b. In the gray row at the end of the form, **double-click the check box form field** to display the Check Box Form Field Options dialog box.

c. In the Run Macro On section, from the Entry drop-down list, **select Print Letter and click OK.**

5. **Test the form, including the print macro.**

   a. **Protect the form with the password,** *password*

   b. **Scroll up** the document to view the top portion of the form.

   c. From the Title drop-down list, **select Mr.**

   d. **Press Tab** to move to the next field and **type** *Miles*

   e. **Press Tab and type** *Rodriguez*

   f. **Fill in the listed information in the appropriate form fields:**
      - Street: *706 Branch Dr*
      - City: *Boston*
      - State: *MA*

   g. In the gray row at the end of the form, **check the check box** to print the letter.

   > If you have entered all of the new client's information and would like to print the introduction letter to the default printer, check this box. ☒

   h. **Scroll down** to view the client details populated in the form letter.

    When the check box is checked, the print macro is triggered. You can see the form being printed in the status bar.

   i. **Reset the form.**

   j. **Password protect the form with the password,** *password*

   k. **Save the file as** *My Printable New Client Form.dotm* **and close the document.**

B | Using XML in Word

Lesson Time: 1 hour(s), 20 minutes

Objectives:

In this lesson, you will use XML in Word.

You will:

- Tag an existing document.
- Transform an XML document.

Introduction

You know how to create forms. For the most part, individual documents are static containers of information, making that information rather difficult to use in other capacities. XML can help alleviate this problem. In this lesson, you will learn how to use XML in Microsoft® Office Word 2007.

You have a document with specific client information that needs to be added to a customer service database. Rather than spending time retyping those details in the database, potentially making data entry mistakes, Word can save that information in a different format that can be used by your database or in other programs.

TOPIC A
Tag an Existing Document

Word can save documents in several file formats, making the entire document available to other programs. However, doing so saves all of the document's contents. You cannot easily save specific information. In this topic, you will mark an existing document so that the information you want can be easily extracted.

You just received a 20-page document, and wherever you see an employee's name, you are expected to copy that name and paste it into the new employee database. There are nearly 100 references to employee names in the long document. If you could simply identify and mark those names and have that information extracted from the document to the database, you could save time and avoid potential mistakes.

XML

Definition:

XML, which stands for Extensible Markup Language, is a way to describe content by providing sets of rules for creating and defining structured text files. XML only describes content using tags; it does not describe the format of the content. Once defined, the data can be exchanged between different systems or programs.

Example:

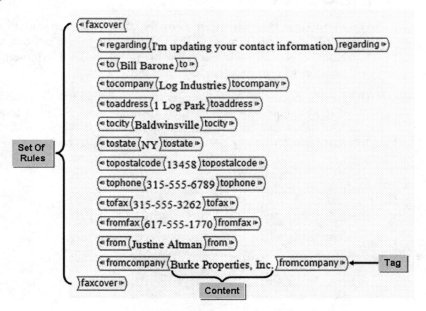

XML Schemas

Definition:

An *XML schema* is a file that contains a set of rules that describe how data can be used in an XML document. Schemas define the data type for the elements and attributes in XML files. Multiple XML files of the same type can use the same schema to validate their structure. XML schemas are saved with the .xsd file extension. You can map the XML elements of the schema to specific content.

Example:

faxcoversheet.xsd

```
<?xml version="1.0" encoding="utf-8" ?>
- <xsd:schema xmlns:xsd="http://www.w3.org/2001/XMLSchema"
    xmlns="http://www.example.com/fax-schema/"
    xmlns:mstns="http://www.example.com/fax-schema/"
    targetNamespace="http://www.example.com/fax-schema/"
    elementFormDefault="qualified" id="faxcoversheet">
    <xsd:element name="faxcover" type="faxtype" />
- <xsd:complexType name="faxtype" mixed="true">          ────▶  Data Type Of Element
  - <xsd:all>
      <xsd:element name="to" type="xsd:string" />
      <xsd:element name="tocompany" type="xsd:string" />
      <xsd:element name="toaddress" type="xsd:string" />
      <xsd:element name="tocity" type="xsd:string" />
      <xsd:element name="tostate" type="xsd:string" />
      <xsd:element name="topostalcode" type="xsd:string" />
      <xsd:element name="tophone" type="xsd:string" />
      <xsd:element name="tofax" type="xsd:string" />
      <xsd:element name="fromfax" type="xsd:string" />
      <xsd:element name="from" type="xsd:string" />
      <xsd:element name="fromcompany" type="xsd:string" />
      <xsd:element name="regarding" type="xsd:string" />
    </xsd:all>
    <xsd:attribute name="senddate" type="xsd:string" />  ◀────  Data Type Of Attribute
  </xsd:complexType>
</xsd:schema>
```

Set of rules describing the usage of data in an XML document

Validation

A schema contains a set of rules that describe what types of data can be used in an XML document and in what order the data must be placed. When Word compares the contents of an XML document to the rules listed in the attached schema, it is called validation. If validation is being enforced and the rules are not followed in the XML document, the violations are displayed in the XML Structure task pane as an icon next to the element name where the violation occurs. To see information about a violation in a ScreenTip, place the mouse pointer over the Violation icon.

 If the Show Advanced XML Error Messages check box is checked in the XML Options dialog box, invalid XML will be represented by a jagged vertical line displayed in the XML document's left margin, and the information displayed in the ScreenTip will be more detailed.

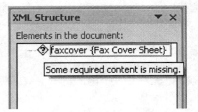

Figure B-1: *An example of a violation.*

XML Elements

Each rule in a schema is called an *element*. An element is a container that consists of a start tag, content, and an end tag. The tags display the name of the element on the screen. The term element is often used synonymously with the term tag.

Attributes

Some of the data stored in an XML document may not be critical to the structure or may not need to be displayed, but it may still be necessary to include that data in the content. In these cases, attributes are used. An *attribute* is a markup component that contains data that further describes the data stored in an element. An attribute is part of an element and is found in both the start tag and the end tag.

The XML Group

The XML group on the Developer tab has various commands that allow you to insert XML files and schemas in Word.

The commands in the XML group are described in the following table.

Command	Description
Structure	Opens the XML Structure task pane.
Schema	Manages the XML schema attached to the document or allows you to add a new schema to the document by displaying the XML Schema tab available in the Templates And Add-Ins dialog box.
Transformation	Transforms the XML files to other document types such as HTML and XML.
Expansion Packs	Manages the XML expansion packs attached to the document or inserts a new expansion pack to the document by displaying the XML Expansion Packs tab available in the Templates And Add-Ins dialog box.

The Schema Library Dialog Box

The Schema Library dialog box provides convenient access to tools used to work with XML documents. In the Schema Library, you can add or delete schemas as well as modify and update schema settings. The Schema Library also contains tools to modify the appearance of XML documents.

Aliases

When you add a schema to the Schema Library, the schema is typically referred to by a lengthy and complicated name that uniquely identifies the schema's contents. Rather than referring to the long name, Word provides you with a way to provide your own user-friendly name, called an alias. You can specify this user-friendly name in the Alias text box available in the Schema Settings dialog box. The schema is then listed by its alias in the Available XML Schemas list box in the Templates And Add-Ins dialog box.

The XML Structure Task Pane

The XML Structure task pane is used to apply XML elements to a Word document. It shows an attached schema and its elements. Mapping, or tagging, a document takes the document's data and maps it to the structure defined by the attached schema.

Hiding XML Tags in the Document

If you find the XML tags distracting, you can hide them by unchecking the Show XML Tags In The Document check box. This hides the tags from view without deleting them. You can then display and hide them, as desired.

XML Options

At the bottom of the XML Structure task pane is a link to XML Options. In the XML Options dialog box, you can modify how an XML document is saved, validated, and viewed. For instance, you can decide whether or not to validate an XML document against its attached schema or to allow the XML document to be saved even if it is not considered to be valid. You can also display the XML Options dialog box from the XML Schema button in the Templates And Add-Ins dialog box.

Word XML Format

When you save an existing document as XML, Word attaches its own schema. The purpose of the schema is to retain Word-related information—the document's properties, original structure, and formatting options—in the XML. As a result, the saved XML document retains its document-like appearance, enabling you to use it either as a Word document or as an XML document.

 The Word XML schema, though attached, is not displayed on either the XML Schema tab or in the Schema Library because you are not allowed to modify it in any way.

How to Tag an Existing Document

Procedure Reference: View XML Documents and Schemas

To view XML documents or schemas in Notepad:

1. In Windows Explorer, navigate to the XML document or schema you want to view.
2. Right-click the XML document or schema, and choose Open With→Notepad.

Procedure Reference: Add a Schema to the Schema Library

To add a schema to the Schema Library:

1. Display the Developer tab.
2. In the XML group, click Schema to display the Templates And Add-Ins dialog box.
3. Display the Add Schema dialog box.
   - On the XML Schema tab, in the Available XML Schemas section, click Add Schema.
   - Or, on the XML Schema tab, in the Available XML Schemas section, click Schema Library and in the Schema Library dialog box, in the Schemas section, click Add Schema.
4. Locate and select the schema file and click Open.
5. If necessary, in the Schema Settings dialog box, in the Alias text box, give the schema a meaningful name.
6. Click OK to close the Schema Settings dialog box.
7. If necessary, click OK to close the Schema Library dialog box.
8. If necessary, in the Available XML Schemas section, in the Checked Schemas Are Currently Attached list box, check the desired schema's check box to attach it to the open document.
9. If necessary, set Schema Validation Options.
   - Check the Validate Document Against Attached Schemas check box to validate the document against the schemas that are attached.
   - Or, check the Allow Saving As XML Even If Not Valid check box to save the document as XML even when the document is not valid.
10. If necessary, delete the schema from the Schema Library.
    a. In the Templates And Add-Ins dialog box, on the XML Schema tab, in the Available XML Schemas section, click Schema Library.
    b. In the Schema Library dialog box, in the Schemas section, in the Select A Schema list box, select the schema you want to delete and click Delete Schema.
    c. Click Yes to remove the schema.
    d. Click OK to close the Schema Library dialog box.
11. Click OK to close the Templates And Add-Ins dialog box.

Procedure Reference: Modify Schema Settings

To modify a schema's settings:

1. Display the Templates And Add-Ins dialog box.
2. On the XML Schema tab, in the Available XML Schemas section, click Schema Library.
3. In the Schema Library dialog box, in the Schemas section, in the Select A Schema list box, select the schema that you want to modify.

4. Click Schema Settings.

5. If necessary, in the Alias text box, type a user-friendly name to refer to the schema that will be displayed in the schema list.

6. If necessary, browse to the schema in a new location and click Open to change the schema's location.

7. Click OK two times.

8. Click OK to close the Templates And Add-Ins dialog box.

Procedure Reference: Tag an Existing Document

To tag an existing document:

1. Attach the schema to the document.

   a. Display the Templates And Add-Ins dialog box.

   b. On the XML Schema tab, in the Available XML Schemas section, in the Checked Schemas Are Currently Attached list box, check the desired schema's check box.

   c. If necessary, set Schema Validation Options.

   d. Click OK.

 To separate a schema from a document, simply uncheck the schema's check box.

2. In the document, select the content to which you want to apply the first element.

3. In the XML Structure task pane, in the Choose An Element To Apply To Your Current Selection list box, select the desired element.

4. If necessary, in the Apply To Entire Document dialog box, specify the desired options.

   • Click Apply To Entire Document to apply the element to the entire document.

   • Or, click Apply To Selection Only to apply the element to the selected text of the document.

5. If necessary, specify the attributes for the applied element.

   a. In the XML Structure task pane, in the Elements In The Document list box, right-click the desired element and choose Attributes.

   b. In the Attributes For [Element] dialog box, in the Available Attributes list box, select the desired attribute.

   c. In the Value text box, type the value for the assigned attribute and click Add.

 If you are creating a template, you can type placeholder text that will be displayed between the tags until a value is entered.

   d. Click OK.

Procedure Reference: Hide the Alias

To hide the alias:

1. Display the XML Options dialog box.

   ● In the Templates And Add-Ins dialog box, on the XML Schema tab, in the Available XML Schemas section, click XML Options.

   ● Or, at the bottom of the XML Structure task pane, click the XML Options link.

2. In the XML View Options section, check the Hide Namespace Alias In XML Structure task pane check box to hide the alias.

3. Click OK.

4. If necessary, remove the tag.

   a. In the XML Structure task pane, verify that the Show XML Tags In Document check box is checked.

   b. Right-click either the start or end of the tag to be removed and choose Remove Tag.

 You can also use the Elements In The Document list box to remove a tag. Right-click the tag you want to remove and choose the element's Remove Tag option.

Procedure Reference: Save a Document as XML

To save a document as XML:

1. Display the Save As dialog box.

2. From the Save As Type drop-down list, select Word 2003 XML Document (*.xml).

3. If necessary, in the Save As dialog box, in the File Name text box, type a name.

4. Click Save.

5. If necessary, in the Microsoft Office Word Compatibility Checker dialog box, click Continue.

Mixed Content in Word XML

Mixed content is any information that is not inside an element. For instance, you may want to keep an untagged paragraph that includes a great product description you wrote. The information is only valuable to you, so it is not tagged. But, leaving the text may violate an attached schema's rules. By checking the Ignore Mixed Content check box in the XML Options dialog box, the untagged information will not be considered a violation. Additionally, in the XML Structure task pane, mixed content will not be displayed in the Elements In The Document list box as a series of three dots.

Data Only

If an XML document is going to be used by other programs, displayed in a different format, or distributed to someone who does not have Word 2003 or higher, you may want to remove all of the document's extraneous formatting and mixed content. This is done by checking the Save Data Only check box available in the XML Save Options section in the XML Options dialog box or in the Save As dialog box. Doing so saves only the content that is tagged with an element.

Procedure Reference: Save a Document as a Data-Only XML File

To save a document as a data-only XML file:

1. Display the XML Options dialog box.
2. In the XML Save Options section, check the Save Data Only check box.

 You can also check the Save Data Only check box in the Save As dialog box when Word 2003 XML Document (*.xml) is the selected file type.

3. If necessary, in the Schema Validation Options section, check the Ignore Mixed Content check box.
4. Click OK to close the XML Options dialog box.
5. If necessary, click OK to close the Templates And Add-Ins dialog box.
6. Display the Save As dialog box.
7. If necessary, in the File Name text box, type a file name.
8. Click Save and close the file.

 The XML Document task pane appears only when you open a data-only XML file.

ACTIVITY B-1

Adding a Schema to the Schema Library

Data Files:

Schema1.xsd, Schema2.xsd

Before You Begin:

A blank document is open.

Scenario:

You have been asked to help update client contact information. Part of the process will be to generate a fax cover sheet from XML data to accompany a letter that will be sent to the client. Before you update the client's contact information, you have to add the fax schema to the Schema Library. But, you find that there are two schemas available and you are not sure which is the fax schema.

What You Do	How You Do It
1. Add Schema1.xsd to the Schema Library.	a. On the Developer tab, in the XML group, **click Schema.**
	b. In the Templates And Add-Ins dialog box, on the XML Schema tab, in the Available XML Schemas section, **click Add Schema.**
	c. In the Add Schema dialog box, **navigate to the C:\084895Data\Appendix B folder, select the Schema1.xsd file, and click Open.**
	d. In the Schema Settings dialog box, notice that the URI field displays the inventory schema—not the fax schema—and **click OK.**
2. Delete Schema1.xsd from the Schema Library.	a. **Click Schema Library** to display the Schema Library dialog box.
	b. In the Schemas section, in the Select A Schema list box, **select http://www.example.com/inventory-schema/ and click Delete Schema.**
	c. In the Schema Library dialog box, **click Yes** to remove the schema.

3. **Add Schema2.xsd to the Schema Library.**

a. In the Schema Library dialog box, **click Add Schema.**

b. In the Add Schema dialog box, **navigate to the C:\084895Data\Appendix B folder, select Schema2.xsd, and click Open.**

c. In the Schema Settings dialog box, notice that the URI field displays the fax schema.

d. In the Alias text box, **type *Fax Cover Sheet* and click OK.**

e. **Click OK** two times.

f. **Close the blank document.**

ACTIVITY B-2

Tagging an Existing Document

Data Files:

Barone Contact Info.docx

Before You Begin:

From the C:\084895Data\Appendix B folder, open Barone Contact Info.docx.

Scenario:

You have added the fax cover sheet schema to the Schema Library. Now, you would like to add the fax cover sheet to the Barone Contact Info document and validate it. Also, you would like to include the current date as the fax cover sheet's Senddate value. Finally, you want to attach the other remaining elements to the document.

What You Do	How You Do It
1. **Apply the Faxcover element to the entire document.**	a. On the Developer tab, in the XML group, **click Schema.**
	b. In the Templates And Add-Ins dialog box, on the XML Schema tab, in the Available XML Schemas section, in the Checked Schemas Are Currently Attached list box, **check the Fax Cover Sheet check box.**
	c. In the Schema Validation Options section, **check the Validate Document Against Attached Schemas check box and click OK.**
	d. **Press Ctrl+A** to select the entire document.
	e. In the XML Structure task pane, in the Choose An Element To Apply To Your Current Selection list box, **select Faxcover {Fax Cover Sheet}.**

 If the {Fax Cover Sheet} alias is hidden, click XML Options and uncheck the Hide Namespace Alias In XML Structure Task Pane check box.

	f. In the Apply To Entire Document dialog box, **click Apply To Entire Document.**

2. Specify a date value for the Faxcover element's Senddate attribute.

a. In the XML Structure task pane, in the Elements In The Document list box, **right-click Faxcover {Fax Cover Sheet} and choose Attributes.**

b. In the Attributes For Faxcover dialog box, in the Available Attributes list box, notice that the Senddate attribute is selected.

c. In the Value text box, **type the current date and click Add.**

d. **Click OK.**

3. Modify the XML Options so that the alias, {Fax Cover Sheet}, is hidden.

a. At the bottom of the XML Structure task pane, **click the XML Options link.**

b. In the XML Options dialog box, in the XML View Options section, **check the Hide Namespace Alias In XML Structure Task Pane check box and click OK.**

4. Complete the tagging of Bill Barone's contact information.

a. In the document's contact information list, **select the text "Bill Barone".**

b. In the XML Structure task pane, in the Choose An Element To Apply To Your Current Selection list box, **select To.**

c. In the document's contact information list, **select the text "Log Industries".**

d. In the XML Structure task pane, in the Choose An Element To Apply To Your Current Selection list box, **select Tocompany.**

e. **Tag the listed text with the appropriate elements:**
   - 1 Log Park: Toaddress
   - Baldwinsville: Tocity
   - NY: Tostate
   - 13458: Topostalcode
   - 315-555-6789: Tophone
   - 315-555-3262: Tofax
   - I'm updating your contact information.: Regarding
   - 617-555-1770: Fromfax
   - Justine Altman: From
   - Burke Properties, Inc.: Fromcompany

5. **Save the XML file as a data-only file without mixed content.**

a. At the bottom of the XML Structure task pane, **click the XML Options link.**

b. In the XML Options dialog box, in the XML Save Options section, **check the Save Data Only check box.**

c. In the Schema Validation Options section, **check the Ignore Mixed Content check box and click OK.**

d. **Display the Save As dialog box.**

e. **From the Save As Type drop-down list, select Word 2003 XML Document (*.xml).**

f. In the File Name text box, **type *My Barone Data***

g. Notice that the Save Data Only check box is checked. **Click Save.**

h. In the Microsoft Office Word Compatibility Checker dialog box, **click Continue.**

i. **Close My Barone Data.xml.**

 It is necessary to close My Barone Data.xml because the data-only aspect is only displayed when the file is reopened.

j. **Navigate to the C:\084895Data\ Appendix B folder and open My Barone Data.xml in Word.**

k. Notice that the file contains no Word formatting, the text that was tagged is included, and the XML Document task pane is displayed.

TOPIC B

Transform an XML Document

Once a document has been saved as XML, it can be used in several different ways. In this topic, you will transform an XML document.

You have a letter saved as an XML document and you need to fax it to a client. Rather than create a new fax cover sheet from the Fax Cover Sheet (Elegant Design) template and re-enter all of that person's personal information, you can just transform the cover letter into the fax cover sheet you need by applying the fax transform that your IT department supplied you.

Transforms

Definition:

A *transform* is an Extensible Stylesheet Language (XSL) file that contains formatting instructions. It can be applied to an XML document to display the tagged data as other types of documents. Transforms can be saved with file extensions .xsl and .xslt. You can apply transforms to the whole document or part of the document.

Example:

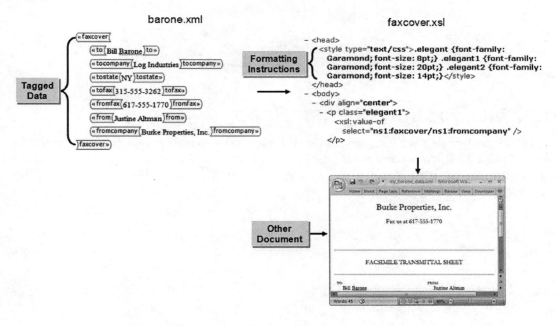

Solutions

Definition:

In Word, a *solution* is a transform that is associated with a particular schema. By adding a transform as a solution to a schema, you make the transform available to any XML document that uses that particular schema. Each schema can have several solutions associated with it.

Example:

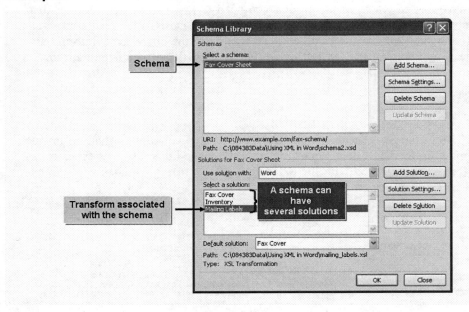

The XML Document Task Pane

The XML Document task pane displays a list of all available transforms and solutions that can be applied to an XML document. It can also be used to browse for additional transforms so the data can be displayed in a different view.

How to Transform an XML Document

Procedure Reference: Apply a Transform to a Data-Only XML File

To apply a transform to a data-only XML file:

1. In the XML Document task pane, below the XML Data Views list box, click Browse.
2. In the XSL Transformation dialog box, locate and select the transform (*.xsl) file and click Open.

Procedure Reference: Apply a Transform to an XML Document While Saving

To apply a transform to an XML document while saving:

1. Display the Save As dialog box.
2. If necessary, rename the file.
3. Check the Apply Transform check box and click Transform.
4. In the Choose An XSL Transformation dialog box, locate and select the desired transform file and click Open.
5. Check the Save Data Only check box and click Save.

Procedure Reference: Open a Data-Only XML File with a Transform

To open a data-only XML file with a transform:

1. Display the Open dialog box.
2. Locate and select the data-only XML file.
3. Click the Open button drop-down arrow and choose Open With Transform.
4. In the Choose An XSL Transformation dialog box, locate and select the desired transform file and click OK.

Procedure Reference: Add a Solution to a Schema

To add a solution to a schema:

1. Display the Templates And Add-Ins dialog box.
2. On the XML Schema tab, click Schema Library.
3. In the Schema Library dialog box, in the Select A Schema list box, select the schema to which you want to add a solution and click Add Solution.
4. In the Add Solution dialog box, locate and select the desired transform file and click Open.
5. If necessary, in the Solution Settings dialog box, in the Alias text box, type an alias and click OK.
6. If necessary, in the Solutions For [Schema] section, from the Default Solution drop-down list, select a default solution.
7. Click OK two times.

8. If necessary, delete the solution.

    a. Display the Templates And Add-Ins dialog box.

    b. On the XML Schema tab, click Schema Library.

    c. Select the schema and the solution you want to delete, and click Delete Solution.

    d. In the Schema Library dialog box, click Yes to confirm that you want to remove the solution from the Schema Library.

    e. Click OK two times.

ACTIVITY B-3

Transforming an XML Document

Data Files:

Fax Cover.xsl, Mailing Labels.xsl, My Barone Data.xml.

Before You Begin:

My Barone Data.xml is open.

Scenario:

Your company's IT department has provided you with two transforms, one to generate a fax cover sheet and the other to generate mailing labels, when applied to tagged data. Now that you have extracted the required data from the letter, you would like to transform the data into a printable fax cover sheet. Also, you want to use the data to generate some mailing labels for the client.

What You Do	How You Do It
1. **Apply the Fax Cover transform to the data.**	a. In the XML Document task pane, below the XML Data Views list box, **click Browse.**
	b. In the XSL Transformation dialog box, **navigate to the C:\084895Data\Appendix B folder, select Fax Cover.xsl, and click Open.**
	c. Notice that the Fax Cover.xsl transform is added to the XML Data Views list box.
	d. **Save the file as *My Faxcover.docx***
2. **Apply the Mailing Labels transform to the data.**	a. **Open My Barone Data.xml** and in the XML Document task pane, below the XML Data Views list box, **click Browse.**
	b. In the XSL Transformation dialog box, **navigate to the C:\084895Data\Appendix B folder, select Mailing Labels.xsl, and click Open.**
	c. **Save the file as *My Mailing Labels.docx***
	d. **Close all open documents.**

ACTIVITY B-4

Adding Solutions to a Schema

Data Files:

Giles Data.xml, Smith Data.xml, Mailing Labels.xsl, Fax Cover.xsl

Before You Begin:

From the C:\084895Data\Appendix B folder, open Giles Data.xml.

Scenario:

Adding transforms to a data-only XML file is useful, but after you close the file, the applied transforms are removed. Since you will be using the Fax Cover transform occasionally and the Mailing Labels transform frequently, it would be convenient if they were available when you open data-only files based on the Fax Cover Sheet schema.

What You Do	How You Do It
1. **Add the Fax Cover.xsl transform to the Fax Cover Sheet schema as a solution.**	a. On the Developer tab, in the XML group, **click Schema.**
	b. In the Templates And Add-Ins dialog box, on the XML Schema tab, **click Schema Library.**
	c. In the Schema Library dialog box, in the Schemas section, in the Select A Schema list box, **select Fax Cover Sheet.**
	d. In the Solutions For Fax Cover Sheet section, **click Add Solution.**
	e. In the Add Solution dialog box, **navigate to the C:\084895Data\Appendix B folder, select Fax Cover.xsl, and click Open.**
	f. In the Solution Settings dialog box, in the Alias text box, **type *Fax Cover* and click OK.**
	g. Similarly, **add the Mailing Labels.xsl transform to the Fax Cover Sheet schema as a solution, with the alias *Mailing Labels***
	h. **Close the Schema Library dialog box and the Templates And Add-Ins dialog box.**

2. **Verify that the solutions are available to other XML files based on the Fax Cover schema.**

   a. **Display the Open dialog box.**

   b. In the Open dialog box, **select Smith Data.xml and click Open.**

   c. Notice that the Fax Cover and Mailing Labels solutions are listed in the XML Data Views list box.

   d. **Close all open files and then close the application.**

Lesson Labs

Due to classroom setup constraints, some labs cannot be keyed in sequence immediately following their associated lesson. Your instructor will tell you whether your labs can be practiced immediately following the lesson or whether they require separate setup from the main lesson content.

Lesson 1 Lab 1

Using Word with Other Programs

Activity Time: 10 minutes

Data Files:

Employee Report.docx, Employee Changes.xls

Before You Begin:

From the C:\084895Data\Using Word 2007 with Other Programs folder, open Employee Report.docx.

Scenario:

Your editor, Mary Coleman, asks you to update the Employee Report document with details from the Employee Change worksheet. She would also like you to create a PowerPoint presentation from the report and email it to her for review.

1. From Employee Changes.xlsx, **copy the Hires and Terminations data and paste a link into the employee transitions chart datasheet so that the chart displays the numbers.**

2. **Insert a linked worksheet object for Employee Changes.xlsx.**

3. **Save the updated report as *My Employee Report.docx* and send it to PowerPoint, saving the new presentation as *My Employee Show.pptx*.**

4. **Email the updated report to Mary Coleman.**

5. **Exit PowerPoint and Excel without saving changes to those files.**

6. **Close My Employee Report.docx.**

Lesson 2 Lab 1

Reviewing Documents

Activity Time: 10 minutes

Data Files:

Review Employee.docx, Updated Mc.docx

Before You Begin:

From the C:\084895Data\Collaborating on Documents folder, open Review Employee.docx and Updated Mc.docx.

Scenario:

You had sent the employee report to Mary Coleman for review. She has reviewed and returned her marked-up copy. You now need to review the tracked changes and accept or reject them with appropriate comments before sending the document for her approval.

---

1. **Merge the Updated Mc.docx document into the Review Employee.docx document.**

---

2. **Review the tracked changes, accepting and rejecting them, as needed.**

---

3. **Save the document as *My Review Employee.docx* and email it back to Mary Coleman.**

Lesson 3 Lab 1

Combining Changes from Different Document Versions

Activity Time: 20 minutes

Data Files:

Newsletter.docx, Newsletter R1.docx, Newsletter R2.docx, Newsletter R3.docx

Before You Begin:

From the C:/084895Data/Managing Document Versions folder, open Newsletter.docx.

You will need a SharePoint server set up to complete this lab.

Scenario:

You had created a newsletter for Burke Properties, a real estate brokerage firm, and uploaded it in the SharePoint server for review and approval. Since you are relatively new to developing content for a newsletter, your document went through extra rounds of reviews. In the future, you hope to avoid these extra reviews by trying not to repeat some of the basic errors you made while working on the newsletter. So, you decide to spend some time studying the edits from different reviewers. But you do not want to waste time checking out and checking in each version one after the other to view the changes from one reviewer at a time.

1.   **Create a new workspace, *Current Projects* , on the SharePoint server and save the Newsletter.docx file to it.**

2.   **Change the versioning settings to enable SharePoint to create a major version of the document each time you check it in.**

3.   **Check out the newsletter document.**

 Use the Newsletter R1.docx, Newsletter R2.docx, and Newsletter R3.docx files to create three new versions of the document with changes from three different reviewers. Finally, check out the document with the changes from the third reviewer, accept all the tracked changes, delete all comments, and then check in the document to another version.

4.   **Check out the latest version of the newsletter document.**

5.   **Open the first, second, third, and fourth versions of the document.**

6.   **Combine changes from the first and second versions.**

7. Combine the changes in the new compared document with the changes in the third version.

8. Combine the new compared document with the changes in the fourth version.

9. Save the second compared document in a local folder on your machine.

Lesson 4 Lab 1

Adding Reference Marks and Notes

Activity Time: 15 minutes

Data Files:

Employee Reference.docx

Before You Begin:

From the 084895Data\Adding Reference Marks And Notes folder, open Employee Reference.docx.

Scenario:

You are in charge of tracking the performance of employees in your organization. Starting with the second quarter, employee reports are to be saved at the end of every month in a single document so that the month-to-month results can be compared. To make it easier to find each month's information, you need to bookmark the monthly reports. You also need to add appropriate captions to the charts and tables so that they can be readily associated with their corresponding month. You now need to provide footnotes explaining variations in employee sales performance and cross-references when referring to other monthly employee reports.

1. Bookmark the April Employee Report, May Employee Report, and June Employee Report headings.

2. Add figure captions to all charts, making sure that each caption contains the proper month of the particular report.

3. Insert table figure captions for all of the tables, making sure that each caption contains the proper month of the particular report.

4. Under the Employee Performance heading, insert footnotes at the end of each month's Sales text, doing your best to explain any monthly variations.

5. In May's employee report, insert cross-references to both the Services and Sales information with the corresponding information in the April report.

6. Save the document as *My Employee Reference.docx* and close it.

Lesson 5 Lab 1

Making Long Documents Easier to Use

Activity Time: 15 minutes

Data Files:

Employee Report Master.docx, Er Jan.docx, Er Feb.docx, Er Mar.docx, Er Apr.docx, Er May.docx, Er Jun.docx, Er Concordance.docx

Before You Begin:

From the C:\084895Data\Making Long Documents Easier To Use folder, open Employee Report Master.docx.

Scenario:

In the past, you created separate monthly employee reports. But now, the management feels that an annual employee report would be easy to refer to. Therefore, you have been asked to include the January through June employee reports as subdocuments in the Employee Report Master document and use the Er Concordance file to mark index entries. You then need to create an index, a list of figures, a list of tables, and a table of contents.

1. In the Employee Report Master document, below the "Tables" title, **insert the Er [month] employee reports as subdocuments.**

2. **AutoMark index entries using the Er Concordance file.**

3. At the end of the master document, **add a single column index with the page numbers right-aligned.**

4. **Insert a one-level table of contents.**

5. **Insert a table of figures.**

6. **Insert a table of tables.**

7. Save and close the document.

Lesson 6 Lab 1

Securing a Document

Activity Time: 10 minutes

Data Files:

Annual Employee Report.docx

Before You Begin:

From the C:\084895Data\Securing a Document folder, open Annual Employee Report.docx.

Scenario:

Even though it is only halfway through the year, you have been unexpectedly asked to furnish the annual employee report. The report's properties need to be updated to reflect the new time frame. The report also contains your conclusions regarding salary increases. These conclusions aren't public knowledge and should remain somewhat private. Since there have been some questions as to who has access to the network location, you need to take measures to secure the document as best you can.

---

1. Open the Annual Employee Report.docx document.

2. In the Summary properties, update the title to read *Six-Month Employee Report*

3. Hide the Six-Month Conclusions text.

4. Update the entire table of contents and index to hide any references to the hidden text.

5. Protect the document so that it cannot be edited.

6. Password protect the document with a password of *password* and save it as *My Annual Employee Report.docx*

7. Verify that the security settings work as specified.

Appendix A Lab 1

Creating Forms

Data Files:

Rental New Client Form.dotx

Before You Begin:

From the C:\084895Data\Appendix A folder, open Rental New Client Form.dotx.

Scenario:

Your manager has asked you to finish the Rental New Client Form template by adding Apartment Type and Rental Terms drop-down form fields, some Monthly Price Range check box form fields, and a Wants/Needs text form field to contain any specific client requirements. Your manager would also like you to add references in the letter to the new form fields to reduce unnecessary typing.

1. Unprotect the Rental New Client Form template with a password of *password.*

2. Insert an Apartment Type drop-down form field that includes: *Studio, 1-Bedroom, 2-Bedroom, 3-Bedroom,* and *4-Bedroom* items.

3. Insert a Rental Terms drop-down form field that includes *Annual Renewal, Long-Term Lease, Month-to-Month,* and *Rent-to-Own* items.

4. Insert Monthly Price Range check box form fields for the following: *<$500, $500–$1,000, $1,000–$1,500* and *>$1,500.*

5. Insert a Wants/Needs text form field so that the client can enter his specific requirements.

6. Create bookmarks for the new form fields.

7. Insert cross-references to the bookmarked fields in the letter's first paragraph.

8. Test the form, password protect it, and save it as *My Rental New Client Form.dotx.*

Appendix B Lab 1

Tagging and Transforming an Existing Document

Data Files:

Classics Memo.docx, Inventory.xsd, Inventory.xsl

Before You Begin:

From the C:\084895Data\Appendix B folder, open Classics Memo.docx.

Scenario:

You received a memo from the main office suggesting some books to promote in your book-store. You need to quickly create an alphabetized inventory check list so that you can assess your current stock to see which of the titles you need to order from the warehouse.

1. Attach the Inventory.xsd schema to the document.

2. Tag the entire memo as inventory.

3. Modify the element's storename attribute to be *Store 54.*

4. Tag the book titles with the title element.

5. Save the document as a data-only XML file without mixed content named *My Inventory.XML.*

6. Apply the Inventory.xsl transform to the data-only file.

7. Save the transformed file as a Word document named *My Inventory Checklist* and close it.

Solutions

Activity 2-5

2. **True or False? The new document with the compared changes opens in a new window.**

   ___ True

   ✓ False

Glossary

attribute
A markup component that contains data that further describes the data stored in an element. An attribute is part of an element and is found in both the start and end tags.

bibliography
A list of references that is usually inserted at the end of a section or document.

bookmark
Markers within a document that enable users to quickly return to a given location.

caption
A phrase that describes an object such as a picture, graphic, equation, or table.

citation
A reference to any legal source of content.

collaboration
An interaction between two or more people working on the same document.

concordance file
A document used to automatically mark index entries in another document.

cross-reference
A phrase that directs the reader to a particular location in a document.

digital signature
A collection of electronic information that can be used to verify the authenticity of a document.

element
A rule in a schema that describes a type of data and how it can be used.

endnote
A reference note inserted at the end of a document section.

footnote
A reference note inserted at the bottom of a page.

form field
A container inserted into a form that is used to collect a specific type of information.

form
A document used to collect information for a particular purpose in a consistent format.

hyperlink
A navigation tool that links content in a document to other specific content, thereby enabling the user to directly navigate to the linked content.

master document
A document that acts as a container for its own content and links to other documents called subdocuments.

Microsoft Office Document Imaging

A feature that is used to view and manipulate scanned documents and digitally received faxes.

Microsoft Office SharePoint Server 2007

A collaboration and content management server that is integrated with the Office 2007 suite.

signature line

A line used to add a digital signature to a document.

Signatures task pane

A pane that lists all the signatures in a document.

solution

A transform that is associated with a particular schema.

source

Reference material from which content is borrowed.

subdocument

A document linked to a master document.

transform

An Extensible Stylesheet Language file containing formatting instructions that can be applied to an XML document to display the tagged data as other types of documents.

versioning

The process of recording and storing changes made to a document over the course of its development.

XML schema

A file that contains a set of rules that describes what data can be used in an XML document and in what order the data must be placed.

XML

(Extensible Markup Language) A way to describe the content of data by providing sets of rules for creating and defining structured text files.

Index

Looking for media files?

They are now conveniently located at www.elementk.com/courseware-file-downloads

Downloading is quick and easy:

1. Visit www.elementk.com/courseware-file-downloads
2. In the search field, type in either the part number or the title
3. Of the courseware titles displayed, choose your title by clicking on the name
4. Links to the data files are located in the middle of the screen
5. Follow the instructions on the screen based upon your web browser

Note that there may be other files available for download in addition to the course files.

Approximate download times:

The amount of time it takes to download your data files will vary according to the file's size and your Internet connection speed. A broadband connection is highly recommended. The average time to download a 10 mb file on a broadband connection is less than 1 minute.